Salvador Allende was elected president of Chile in 1970 as a member of the Popular Unity Coalition. Less than 3 years later, he was dead, the result of a US-sponsored coup. The coup ushered in the horrific Pinochet regime, the effects of which are still felt today in Chile.

While all of that is well known, Allende's accomplishments, ideology and lifetime of revolutionary struggle are mostly forgotten. Allende was a longtime member of Chile's Soclaist Party, (*Partido Socialista de Chile*, PS), serving as it's secretary in 1943 and serving as Senator for 15 years under that banner. He ran for President 3 times, unsuccessfully, before his 4th and successful run in 1970.

Allende ran under the Popular Unity Coalition in 1970 (Unidad Popular, UP) which united Socialists, Communists, Marxist-Leninists, followers of Liberation Theology and Social Democrats. Although many called for armed revolution, Communists pushed for Allende, believing in his integrity as a Marxist activist, doctor and socialist politician. Their faith was rewarded. Allende enacted several radical reforms, raising working class wages, lowering inflation, promoting gender equality, building emergency housing, granting free education to Chilean's Indigenous population and nationalizing several resources and industries.

Chile was rich with copper, and nationalizing that industry enraged the empire of the United States. They had never liked Allende, openly intervening in his previous electoral runs, trying to scare voters off from electing the socialist. Even after he was democratically elected in 1970, the United States pushed for Congressmembers of Chile to call for new elections.

Allende tried to keep peaceful, cordial relations with the United States, even through his support of Cuba, his rejection of the OAS and his condemnation of other coups throughout the hemisphere But nationalizing copper was a bridge to far for the United States. In September of 1973, Pinochet, the CIA and the Chilean Military carried out a coup, leading to Allende's death.

The United States propped Pinochet up as dictator of Chile for over 15 years, committing unspeakable atrocities in that period. Because Allende's term lasted less than 3 years, it's easy to see why Pinochet's brutality has become intertwined with Allende's lasting legacy.

But in that short time, Allende showed how a radical, planned, socialist economy can transform a country, pull it out of poverty and bring hope and light to the people. His words, his courage and his actions should stand alone as a beacon of light for Latin America. Although it is important to condemn the United States and Pinochet's actions,

Allende's own accomplishments and life should be celebrated.

This collection of speeches hopes to illuminate and preserve that legacy.

Salvador Allende 1970

Victory Speech

Speech delivered on the morning of September 5th, 1970, from the balcony of the building of the Federation of Chilean Students in Santiago. Translated: by Marianela D'Aprile.

I am deeply moved as I speak to you from this platform, through these subpar speakers. How significant – more so than words – is the presence of the people of Santiago, who, representing the vast majority of Chileans, congregate here to reaffirm the victory that we won fair and square today, a victory that opens a new road for our country, and whose principal actor is the working class of Chile who are gathered here today. How extraordinarily significant it is that today, I can address the people of Chile and the people of Santiago from the Federation of Students. This is of very high value and significance. No candidate who has won thanks to the will and sacrifice of the people has ever used a platform of greater importance. Because we all know: the youth of this country were the vanguard in this great battle, which was not the battle of a single man, but rather the battle of an entire people; this is Chile's victory, reached fairly this afternoon.

I ask you to understand that I am only a man, with every shortcoming and weakness that any man has; and if I was able to endure yesterday's defeat, today, without arrogance and without any spirit of revenge, I accept this victory, which is not personal and which I owe to the united popular parties, to the social forces that have been with us all along. I owe it to the radicals, the socialists, the communists, the social democrats, the members of the MAPU and the API, and to thousands of independents. I owe it to the anonymous and selfless countryman; I owe it to the humble woman of our land. I owe this victory to the working class of Chile, which will come with me into La Moneda on the 4th of November.

The victory you reached today has a deep national meaning. I want to make clear right now that I will respect the rights of all Chileans. But I also want to make clear, and I want you all to know for sure, that as soon as we get to La Moneda, with the working class in power, we will fulfill the historic promise that we've made: to make reality the political program put forth by Unidad Popular.

I've said it before: our purpose is not, nor could it ever be, petty revenge. Nor could we ever, for any reason, give up on or trade the program put forth by Unidad Popular, which was the banner carried the first authentically democratic, popular, national, and revolutionary government in the history of Chile.

I've it said before, and I will say it again: victory wasn't easy, and it will be just as difficult to consolidate our victory and build a new society, a new social contract, a new morality, and a new nation.

But I know that you, you who put the working class in power, will have the historic task of making reality what Chile longs for: to turn our nation into a country peerless in its progress, in its social justice, in the rights of each man, each woman, each young person of our land.

We've triumphed in order to go on to definitively defeat imperialist exploitation, to end with monopolies, to bring about a deep and serious agrarian reform, to control the commerce of imports and exports, to nationalize debt, all pillars that will make possible Chile's progress, creating the social capital that will drive our development.

That's why, this evening, which belongs to History, and in this moment of celebration, I express my deeply felt appreciation to every man and woman, to the militants of the popular parties and the members of the social forces that made this victory possible, and who have aims that go beyond the borders of our own nation.

To those in the pampas or in the steppes, to those who are listening from the coast, to those who labor in the foothills of the Andes, to the simple homemaker, to the university professor, to the young student, the small business owner, to every man and woman in Chile, to the youth of our land, to all of them, the promise that I make today, before my conscience and before the working class – the fundamental actor in this victory – is to be authentically loyal in our common and collective task. I've said it before: my only wish is for me to be, in your eyes, your comrade who is president.

The anonymous man, the ignored woman of Chile, it is they who have made possible this most important social event. Thousands and thousands of Chileans sowed their pain and their hope in this moment which belongs to the people. From beyond these borders, from other countries, people look with deep satisfaction onto our victory. Chile is opening a path that other peoples across America and the world will be able to follow. The vital power of unity will break the dams of dictatorships and open the course for other peoples to be free and to build their own destiny.

We are sensible enough to understand that each country and each nation has its own problems, its own history, and its own reality. Facing that reality, the political leaders of those countries will be the ones who decide which tactics to adopt. We can only have the best relationships – political, cultural, economic – with every country in the world. We only ask that they respect – there will be no choice but to do so – the right of the people of Chile to have won for themselves the government of Unidad Popular.

We respect and will respect self-determination and non-intervention. But that does not mean that we will shrink in our alliance in solidarity with peoples fighting for their economic independence and for the dignity of human life across every continent.

I only want to carry out before history the significant event that you all have made reality, defeating the arrogance of money, the threat and pressure that come with it; defeating warped information, a campaign of terror, of malice and insidiousness. If a people has been capable of this, it will also be capable of understanding that only by working more, by producing more, will we be able to make Chile progress and give the man and woman of our land their genuine rights: to work, to housing, to health, to education, to rest, to culture, and to recreation.

We will put all of our creative power in tension to realize the goals laid out by the program of Unidad Popular.

Together, with your efforts, we will bring about the changes that Chile asks for and needs. We will make a revolutionary government.

Revolution does not imply destruction, but rather construction; it doesn't imply demolition, but rather building; and the people of Chile are ready for this great task in this most significant moment of our lives.

Comrades, friends: How I wish that the media had allowed me to talk more at length with all of you, and that each of you had heard my words, steeped in feeling, but at the same time firm in their conviction to the great task that lies before all of us and that I fully take on. I ask that this unprecedented demonstration become the manifestation of the conscience of the people.

You will go back to your houses without the least bit of provocation and without allowing yourselves to be provoked. The people know that their problems are not solved by breaking windows or smashing a car. Those who said that in the future, disturbances like these would characterize our victory, will be met by your conscientiousness and your responsibility. You'll go to work tomorrow or on Monday, happy and singing; singing to this victory so legitimately won, and singing to the future. With the calloused hands of the people and the laughter of children, we will make possible the great task that only a conscientious and disciplined people will be able to carry out.

Latin America and beyond look to our future. I have full faith that we will be strong enough, strong and serene enough, to open up a charmed path toward a different and better life; to start to walk through the hopeful boulevards of socialism that the people of Chile with their own hands will build.

I reiterate my grateful acknowledgement of the militants of Unidad Popular; of the members of the Radical, Communist, Socialist, Social Democratic, MAPU and API parties; and of the thousands of leftist independents who have been with us all along. I express my affection and also my gratitude to the comrades who are leaders of those parties, who – beyond the borders of their own organizations – made possible the strength of the unity claimed by the working class. It's because the working class claimed this unity that our victory, the victory of the people, was possible.

The fact that we are hopeful and happy does not mean that we are going to neglect our vigilance: this weekend, the people will grab the nation by the waist, and we will dance from Arica to Magallanes, from the mountains to the sea, one big cueca, as a symbol of the wholesome joy of our victory.

But at the same time, we will keep our popular action committees vigilant, so that we may be ready to respond to any call – if it were necessary – made by the leadership of Unidad Popular. They will call on the committees of companies, of factories, of hospitals, of neighborhood associations, on the proletarian population, to study our problems and their solutions, because we will quickly have to set the country in motion. I have faith, deep faith, in the honesty and in the heroic conduct of each woman and each man who made this victory possible.

We are going to work more. We are going to produce more.

But we will work more for the Chilean family, for the working class and for Chile, with the pride that we have as Chileans and with the belief that we are carrying out a grand and marvelous historic task. In the deepest fibers of my being, in the human depths of my fighting soul, I feel what each of you gives to me. What is germinating today is part of a long journey. I merely take in my hands the torch lit by those who, long before us, fought alongside the working class and for the working class.

We must make this victory a tribute in honor of those who have fallen in social battles and nourished with their blood the fertile seed of the Chilean revolution that we will carry out.

Before I finish, I want to acknowledge – it's only honest to do it this way – that the government put forth numbers and data accurate to the results of the election. I want to acknowledge that the head of the square, General Camilo Valenzuela, authorized this mass act, with the belief and certainty, assured by me, that the people would congregate responsibly, knowing that they have won the right to be respected in their life and in their victory; the people know that they will come with me into La Moneda on the 4th of November of this year.

I want to highlight that our opponents in Democracia Cristiana have recognized the victory of the people. We will not ask the right to do the same. We don't need to. We don't have any petty feelings against them. But the right will never be able to recognize the greatness of the people in their fight, born of their pain and of their hope.

I've never felt such human warmth as I do now; nor has our national song ever had – for you or for me – as deep a significance as it does now. We've said it before: we are the legitimate heirs of the fathers of the nation, and together we will bring about our second independence: the economic independence of Chile.

Citizens of Santiago, workers of this nation: you and only you are the victors. The popular parties and the social forces have taught us this great lesson, which has repercussions far beyond our material borders.

I ask that you go home with the wholesome joy of a fair victory. Tonight, as you hold your children, as you look to rest, think of the difficult tomorrow that lies ahead of us, when we will have to put forth even more passion, even more care, to make

Chile ever greater, and to make life in our country ever more just.

Thank you, thank you, comrades. I've said it before: my party, the unity of workers, and the unity of the people are the best thing I have.

To your loyalty, I will give back the loyalty of a leader of the people – the loyalty of your comrade who is president.

Salvador Allende 1970

First speech to the Chilean parliament after his election

Introduction

Appearing before you in fulfillment of the constitutional mandate, I attribute twofold importance to this message. It is the first message of a Government which has just taken office, and it corresponds to unique demands in our political history.

For this reason I wish to give it special substance, because of its present significance and because of its implications for the future.

For 27 years, I have attended this House, nearly always as a member of the parliamentary opposition. Today I attend as Chief of State, elected by the will of the people as ratified by Congress.

I am well aware that here were debated and established the laws which set up an agrarian structure based on big estates; but here too, obsolete institutions were abolished in order to lay the legal foundations of the land reform which we are now carrying out. Here were established the institutional procedures for the foreign exploitation of Chilean national resources; but this same Congress is now revising these in order to return to the Chilean people what belongs to them by right.

Congress makes the legal institutions which regulate the social order in which they are rooted; for this reason, for more than a century, it has been more responsive to the interests of the powerful than to the suffering of the people.

At the very commencement of this legislative period, I must raise this problem. Chile now has in its Government a new political force whose social function is to uphold, not the traditional ruling class, but the vast majority of the people. This change in the power structure must necessarily be accompanied by profound changes in the socio-economic order, changes which Parliament is summoned to institutionalize.

This step forward in the liberation of Chilean energies for the rebuilding of the nation must be followed by more decisive steps. The land reform which is now in progress, the nationalizationof copper which is only awaiting the approval of Plenary Congress, must be followed by new reforms - whether these are initiated by Parliament or by Government proposal, or by the combined efforts of both powers, or by plebiscite, which is a legal appeal to the foundation of all power, the sovereignty of the people.

We have accepted the challenge to re-examine everything. We urgently wish to ask of every law, every existing institution and even of every person whether or not they are furthering our integral and autonomous development. I am sure that on few occasions in history has the Parliament of any nation been presented with so great a challenge.

Overcoming Capitalism in Chile

The circumstances of Russia in 1917 and of Chile at the present time are very different. Nevertheless, the historic challenge is similar.

In 1917, Russia took decisions which have had the most far-reaching effects on contemporary history. There it was believed that backward Europe could face up to advanced Europe, that the first socialist revolution need not necessarily take place in the heart of industrial power. There the challenge was accepted and the dictatorship of the proletariat, which is one of the methods of building a socialist society, was established.

Today nobody doubts that by this method nations with a large population can, in a relatively short period, break out of their backwardness and attain the most advanced level of contemporary civilisation. The examples of the Soviet Union and of the Chinese People's Republic speak for themselves.

Like Russia then, Chile now faces the need to initiate new methods of constructing a socialist society. Our revolutionary method, the pluralist method, was anticipated by the classic Marxist theorists but never before put into practice. Social thinkers believed that the first to do so would be the more developed nations, probably Italy or France with their powerful Marxist-oriented working-class parties.

Nevertheless, once again, history has permitted a break with the past and the construction of a new model of society, not only where it was theoretically most predictable but where the most favourable concrete conditions had been created for its achievement. Today Chile is the first nation on earth to put into practice the second model of transition to a socialist society.

This challenge is awakening great interest beyond our national frontiers. Everybody knows or guesses that here and now history is beginning to take a new direction, even as we Chileans are conscious of the undertaking. Some among us, perhaps the minority, see the enormous difficulties of the task. Others, the majority, are trying to envisage the possibility of facing it successfully. For my part, I am sure that we shall have the necessary energy and ability to carry on our effort and create the first socialist society built according to a democratic, pluralistic and libertarian model.

The sceptics and the prophets of doom will say that it is not possible. They will say that a parliament that has served the ruling classes so well cannot be transformed into the Parliament of the Chilean People.

Further, they have emphatically stated that the Armed Forces and the Corps of Carabineros, who have up to the present supported the institutional order that we wish to overcome, would not consent to guarantee the will of the people if these should decide on the establishment of socialism in our country. They forget the patriotic conscience of the Armed Forces and the Carabineros, their tradition of professionalism and their obedience to civil authority. In the words of General Schneider, the Armed Forces are "an integral and representative part of the nation as well as of the State structure, that is, they belong both to the permanent and the temporary spheres, and are therefore able to organize and counter-balance the periodic changes which affect political life within a legal regime". Since the National Congress is based on the people's vote, there is nothing in its nature which prevents it from changing itself in order to become, in fact, the Parliament of the People. The Chilean Armed Forces and the Carabineros, faithful to their duty and to their tradition of non-intervention in the political process, will support a social organization which corresponds to the will of the people as expressed in the terms of the established Constitution. It will be a more just, a more humane and generous organization for everybody, but above all for the workers, who have contributed so much up to the present and have received almost nothing in return.

The difficulties we face are not in this field. They reside in the extraordinary complexity of the tasks before us - to create the political institutions which will lead to Socialism, and to achieve this starting from our present condition of a society oppressed by backwardness and poverty which are the result of dependence and under- development - to break with the factors which cause backwardness and, at the same time, to build a new socio-economic structure capable of providing for collective prosperity.

The causes of backwardness resided and still reside in the traditional ruling classes with their combination of dependence on external forces and internal class exploitation. They have profited from their association with foreign interests, and from their appropriation of the surplus produced by the workers, to whom they have only awarded the minimum indispensable for the renewal of their labouring capacities.

Our first task is to dismantle this restrictive structure, which only produces a deformed growth. At the same time, we must build up a new economy so that it succeeds the previous one without continuing it, at the same time conserving to the maximum the productive and technical capacity that we have achieved despite the vicissitudes of our under- development - and we must build it up without crises artificially provoked by those whose ancient privileges we shall abolish.

In addition to these basic questions, there is another which is an essential challenge of our time - how can people in general - and young people in particular - develop a sense of mission which will inspire them with a new joy in living and give dignity to their existence?

There is no other way than that of devoting ourselves to the realization of great impersonal tasks, such as that of attaining a new stage in the human condition, until now degraded by its division into the privileged and the dispossessed. Today nobody can imagine solutions for the distant future when all nations will have attained abundance and realised the satisfaction of material needs and at the same time have assumed the cultural heritage of humanity. But here and now in Chile and in Latin America, we have the possibility and the duty of releasing creative energies, particularly those of youth, in missions which inspire us more than any in the past. Such is the aspiration to build a world which does away with divisions into rich and poor - and for our part, to build a society in which the war of economic competition is outlawed - in which the struggle for professional privileges has no meaning - in which there is no longer that indifference to the fate of others which permits the powerful to exploit the weak.

There have been few occasions in which men have needed so much faith in themselves and in their capacity to rebuild the world and regenerate their lives.

This is an unprecedented time, which offers us the material means of realizing the most generous utopian dreams of the past. The only thing that prevents our achieving this is the heritage of greed, of fear and of obsolete institutional traditions. Between our time and that of the liberation of man on a planetary scale, this inheritance has to be overcome. Only in this way will it be possible to call upon men to reconstruct their lives, not as products of a past of slavery and exploitation, but in the most conscious realization of their noblest potentialities. This is the socialist ideal.

An ingenious observer from some developed country which has these material resources might suppose that this observation is a new manner that backward people have found of asking for aid - yet another plea of the poor for the charity of the rich. Such is not the case, but its opposite. With the internal authority of all societies brought under the hegemony of the dispossessed, with the change in international trade relations stimulated by the exploited nations, there will come about not only the abolition of poverty and backwardness but also the liberation of the great powers from their despot's fate. Thus, in the same way as the emancipation of the slave liberates the slaveowner, so the achievement of Socialism envisaged by the peoples of our time is as meaningful for the disinherited peoples as for the more privileged, since both will then cast away the chains which degrade their society.

I stand here, members of the National Congress, to urge you to take up the task of reconstructing the Chilean nation according to our dreams, a Chile in which all children begin life equally, with equal medical care, education, and nutrition. A Chile in which the creative ability of each man and woman is allowed to develop, not in competition with others, but in order to contribute to a better life for all.

Our road to Socialism

To achieve these aspirations means a long road and a great effort on the part of all Chileans. It also implies, as a basic prerequisite, that we are able to establish the institutional apparatus of a new form of pluralistic, free socialist order. The task is one of extraordinary complexity because there are no precedents for us to follow. We are treading a new path. We are advancing without guides across unknown territory, but our compass is our faith in the humanism of all ages and particularly in Marxist humanism. Our aim is the establishment of the society that we want, the society which answers the deep-rooted desires of the Chilean people.

For a long time, science and technology have made it possible to assure that everybody enjoys those basic necessities which today are enjoyed only by a minority. The difficulties are not technical, and - in our case at least - they are not due to a lack of national resources. What prevents the realization of our ideals is the organization of society, the nature of the interests which have so far dominated, the obstacles which dependent nations face. We must concentrate our attention on these structures and on these institutional requirements.

Speaking frankly, our task is to define and put into practice, as the Chilean road to socialism, a new model of the State, of the economy and of society which revolves around man's needs and aspirations. For this we need the determination of those who have dared to reconsider the world in terms of a project designed for the service of man. There are no previous experiments that we can use as models - we shall have to develop the theory and practice of new forms of social, political and economic organization, both in order to break with under-development and create socialism.

We can achieve this only on condition that we do not overshoot or depart from our objective. If we should forget that our mission is to establish a social plan for man, the whole struggle of our people for socialism will become simply one more reformist experiment. If we should forget the concrete conditions from which we start in order to try and create immediately something which surpasses our possibilities, then we shall also fail.

We are moving towards socialism, not from an academic love for a doctrinaire system, but encouraged by the strength of our people, who know that it is an inescapable demand if we are to overcome backwardness and who feel that a socialist regime is the only way available to modern nations who want to build rationally in freedom, independence and dignity. We are moving towards socialism because the people, through their vote, have freely rejected capitalism as a system which has resulted in a crudely unequal society, a society deformed by social injustice and degraded by the deterioration of the very foundations of human solidarity.

In the name of the socialist reconstruction of Chilean society, we have won the presidential elections, a victory that was confirmed by the election of municipal councillors. This is the flag behind which we are mobilising the people politically both as the object of our plans and as the justification for our actions. Our Government plans are those of the Popular Unity platform on which we fought the election. In putting them into effect, we shall not sacrifice attention to the present needs of the Chilean people in favour of gigantic schemes. Our objective in none other than the progressive establishment of a new structure of power, founded on the will of the majority and designed to satisfy in the shortest possible time the most urgent needs of the present generation.

Sensitivity to the claims of the people is in fact the only way we have of contributing to the solution of the great human problems - for no universal value is worth the name if it cannot be applied on the national or regional scale and even to the local living conditions of each family.

Our policy might seem too simple for those who prefer big promises. But the people need decent housing for their families, with proper sanitation - they need schools for their children which are not expressly intended for the poor - they need enough to eat every day of the year - they need work - they need care during sickness and in old age - they need to be respected as people. That is what we hope to offer all Chileans in the foreseeable future. This is what has been denied the people in Latin America throughout the centuries. This is what some nations are now beginning to guarantee their entire population.

But beyond this task, and as a fundamental prerequisite for its achievement, there is another equally important one. It is to engage the will of the Chilean people to dedicate our hands, our minds and our feelings to the reassertion of our identity as a people, in order to become an integral part of contemporary civilisation as masters of our fate and heirs to the patrimony of technical skills, knowledge, art and culture. Turning the nation's attention to these fundamental aspirations is the only way to satisfy the people's needs and to wipe out the differences between them and the privileged classes. Above all, it is the only way to provide the young with a mission by opening up broad perspectives of a fruitful existence as builders of the society in which they will live.

The mandate entrusted to us embraces all the nation's material and spiritual resources. We have reached a point at which retreat or a standstill would mean an irreparable national catastrophe. It is my obligation at this time, as the one primarily responsible for the fate of Chile, to indicate clearly the road which we are taking and the dangers and hopes which it offers.

The Popular Government knows that the transcendence of a historical period is determined by social and economic factors which have already been shaped by this same period. These factors embrace the agents and modes of historical change. To ignore this would be to go against the nature of things.

In the revolutionary process which we are living through, there are five essential points upon which we shall concentrate our social and political campaign - the principle of legality, the development of institutions, political freedom, the prevention of violence, and the socialization of the means of production. These are questions which affect the present and future of every citizen.

The principle of legality

Legality is a governing principle today in Chile. It has been achieved as a result of the struggle of many generations against absolutism and the arbitrary exercise of State power. It is an irreversible achievement for as long as differences exist between rulers and ruled.

It is not the principle of legality which the mass movements are protesting against. We are protesting against a legal system whose basic assumptions reflect an oppressive social order. Our legal norms and the regulating machinery of Chilean social relationships correspond at the present time to the needs of the capitalist system. In the transition to socialism, legal norms will correspond to the needs of a people engaged in building a new society. But there will be legality.

Our legal system must be modified. Hence the great responsibility of the two Houses at the present time - to help and not to hinder the changes in this system. On whether the Congress takes a realistic attitude depends to a great extent whether capitalist legality will be succeeded by socialist legality in conformity with the social and economic changes we are making and without a violent break in jurisdiction which would open the door to arbitrary acts and excesses which we, as responsible people, wish to avoid.

Development of institutions

The obligation to organize and govern society according to the rule of law is inherent in our system of institutions. The struggle of the popular movements and parties which are now in the Government has contributed greatly to one of the most promising situations obtained in this country. We have an open system which has defied even those who would seek to infringe upon the will of the people.

The flexibility of our institutions allows us to hope that they will not be a bitter bone of contention. And that, like our legal system, they will adapt to new needs in order to give rise, by constitutional means, to the new institutions required by the overthrow of capitalism.

The new institutions will conform to the principle which justifies and guides our actions, that is, the transference of political and economic power to the workers and to the people as a whole. In order to make this possible, the first priority is the socialization of the basic means of production.

At the same time, political institutions must be adjusted to this new situation. For this reason we shall, at an opportune moment, submit to the sovereign will of the people the necessity of replacing the present Constitution, with its liberal foundations, by a Constitution of a socialist nature and of replacing the bicameral system by a single House.

It is in accordance with this that we have committed ourselves in our Government programme to the realization of our revolutionary task while respecting the rule of law. It is not simply a formal commitment but an explicit recognition that the principles of legality and institutional order are inseparable from a socialist regime despite the difficulties involved in the transitional period.

To maintain these institutions while changing their class basis during this difficult period is an ambitious undertaking of decisive importance for the new social order. Nevertheless, its achievement does not depend solely on our will. It will depend fundamentally on the planning of our social and economic structure, on its short-term evolution and on the degree of realism shown by our people in their political action. At the moment we believe that it is possible, and we are acting upon that assumption.

Political freedom

It is also important to remember that for us, as representatives of the popular forces, political freedom represents the achievement of the people on the difficult road to emancipation. It is an element of real achievement in the historical period that we are now leaving behind. And for this reason, freedom must remain. That is why we respect freedom of conscience for all creeds. That is why we are happy to underline the words of the Cardinal Archbishop of Santiago, Raul Silva Henriquez, in his message to the workers - "The Church which I represent is the Church of Jesus, the son of a carpenter. It began as such, and as such we go on loving it. Its greatest sorrow is that people believe it has forgotten its cradle, which is among the humble".

But we would not be revolutionaries if we limited ourselves simply to preserving political freedom. The Popular Unity Government will strengthen political liberties. It is not sufficient to proclaim them verbally, because this makes them a source of frustration or mockery. We shall make them real, tangible, and concrete, and practicable in the process of achieving economic freedom.

In consequence, the Popular Government bases its policy on a premise which some people artificially reject, that is, on the existence of social classes and sectors with opposing and mutually exclusive interests, and on the existence of unequal political levels within the same class or group.

In the face of this diversity, our Government is concerned with the interests of all those who earn their living by their own labour - workers, members of the professions, technicians, artists, intellectuals, and white-collar workers. These are a group which is growing as a result of capitalist development and becoming more united because of its members' common condition as wage-earners. For the same reason, the Government gives protection to both the small and the medium-sized business sectors, that is, to all sectors which, to a greater or lesser extent, are exploited by the minority who hold the centres of power.

The multi-party coalition of the Popular Government corresponds to this reality. And in the daily confrontation of its interests with those of the ruling classes, it uses the techniques of bargaining and agreement established by the legal system, recognizing at the same time the political freedom of the opposition and keeping its own actions within institutional limitations. Political freedom represents the achievement of the entire Chilean people as a nation.

As President of the Republic, I have fully ratified all these principles of action, which are supported by our revolutionary political theory, conform to the present national situation, and are included in the programme of the Popular Unity Government.

They form part of our plan for developing to the maximum the political potentialities of our country so that the stage of transition towards socialism will be characterized by the selective overcoming of the present system. This will be achieved by destroying or abandoning its negative and oppressive features and by strengthening and broadening its positive features.

Violence

The Chilean people are achieving political power without having used arms. They are taking the road of social emancipation having had to fight only the limitations of a liberal democracy and not a despotic or dictatorial regime. Our people legitimately hope to go through the stage of transition to socialism without having recourse to authoritarian forms of government.

Our wishes are very clear on this point. But the responsibility for guaranteeing the political evolution towards socialism does not reside only in the government and in those movements and parties which it comprises. Our people have stood up to the institutionalized violence which the present capitalist system has held over them. And it is for this reason we are changing the basis of that system.

My government owes its existence to the popular will freely expressed. It answers to this alone. The movements and parties which are included in it give direction to the revolutionary conscience of the masses and express the people's interests. At the same time, they are directly responsible to the people.

Nevertheless, it is my duty to warn you that a danger may threaten the straight road to emancipation and could radically alter the direction which our situation and our collective conscience have marked out for us. This danger is violence directed against the people's determination.

Should violence from within or without, should violence in any form, whether physical, economic, social or political, happen to threaten our normal development and the achievement of our workers, then the integrity of our institutions, the rule of law, political freedom and pluralism will be put in the greatest danger. The fight for social emancipation and for the free determination of our people would necessarily take a different form from that which we, with legitimate pride and historical realism, call the Chilean road to socialism. The determined attitude of the Government and the revolutionary energy of the people, the democratic resolution of the Armed Forces and the Carabineros, will see that Chile advances surely along the road to emancipation.

The unity of the popular forces and the good sense of the middle sectors give us the necessary superiority to prevent the privileged minority from having recourse to violence. If violence is not released against the people, we shall be able to change the basic structures on which the capitalist system rests into a democratic, pluralistic and free society, and to do this without unnecessary physical force, without institutional disorder, without disorganizing production, and at a speed which the Government will determine according to the needs of the people and the level of development of our resources.

Attainment of social freedom

Our aim is the attainment of social freedom through the exercise of political freedom, and this requires the establishment of economic equality as a basis. This is the road which the people have decided upon because they know that the revolutionary transformation of a social system must go through intermediate stages. A revolution that is simply political may consume itself in a few weeks. A social and economic revolution takes years. Time is necessary for the conscience of the masses to be penetrated, for new structures to be organized and made operable as well as to be adapted to the existing ones. It is sheer utopianism to imagine that the intermediary stages can be skipped. It is not possible to destroy a social and economic structure and existing social institutions without at least having first developed a replacement. If the natural exigencies of historical change are not recognized, then reality will remind us of them.

We are very well aware of the lesson of victorious revolutions, the revolutions of those countries which, faced with foreign pressure and civil war, had to speed up their social and economic revolution in order not to fall back into bloody despotism and counter-revolution. Only recently, decades afterwards, have they organized the necessary structures for the definitive overthrow of the previous regime.

The direction which my Government has planned takes into account these facts. We know that to change the capitalist system while respecting law, institutions and political freedoms demands that we confine within certain limits our actions in the economic, political and social fields. This is perfectly well known to every Chilean. These limits are indicated in the Government programme which is being carried out resolutely and without concessions, and in the manner and at the speed which we have previously made known.

The Chilean people, showing their increasing maturity and organization, have entrusted the Popular Government with the defense of their interests. This forces the Government to act on the basis of its total identification and integration with the masses whose will it interprets and directs, and prevents it from growing away from the masses and acting in a dilatory or precipitate manner. Today more than ever, the accord between the people, the popular parties and the Government must be precise and dynamic.

Every historical change corresponds to conditions established at previous stages and creates the elements and agents which are to follow. To pass the transitional stage without restriction of their political liberties, withstage without restriction of their political liberties, without having a legal or institutional vacuum, is a right and a legitimate demand of our people, its full material realization in concrete terms being presumed in a socialist society. The Popular Government will fulfil its responsibility at this decisive time.

The principal constructive agent of the new regime consists in the organization and the conscience of our people, in permanent mobilization in different forms, according to the objective needs of each moment.

We hope that this responsibility, which is not necessarily that of the Government alone, is shared by the Christian Democratic Party, which must demonstrate consistency in adhering to the principles and programmes which it has so often laid before the country.

Socialization of the means of production

In 6 months of Government, we have acted with decision on all fronts. Our economic work has been aimed at breaking down the barriers which impede the complete fulfilment of our material and human potentialities. In 6 months of

Government, we have advanced energetically along the path of irrevocable change. The printed statement which we have just distributed gives a full and detailed account of our activities.

Chile has begun the definitive recovery of our most fundamental source of wealth - copper. The nationalization of our copper is not an act of vengeance or hatred directed towards any group, government or nation. We are, on the contrary, positively exercising an inalienable right on behalf of a sovereign people - that of the full enjoyment of our national resources exploited by our national labour and effort. The recovery of copper is a decision by the whole of Chile, and we demand that all countries and governments respect the unanimous decision of a free people. We shall pay for the copper if it is right to pay, and we shall not pay if it is unjust. We shall watch over our interests. But we shall be implacable if we find out that negligence or fraudulent activity on the part of any persons or entities has harmed the country.

We have nationalized another of our basic resources - iron. A short time ago, negotiations with the Bethlehem corporation were concluded, and as a result, iron mining passed over completely to public ownership. We are now studying the constitution of the national steel complex which will group 6 companies together around the CAP (Pacific Steel Industry). The agreement with North American industry has once again shown that the Government is offering a fair settlement to foreign capital without sacrificing the fundamental interests of our nation. But we are not prepared to tolerate the contempt for our laws and the lack of respect for established authority that we find in some foreign firms. We have also taken over coal as collective property (via the Development Corporation).

The nitrate resources are also ours. According to a settlement by the previous government, we owed $24m in debentures payable in 15 years, which with interest amounts to $38m. The shares belonging to the North American sector were theoretically worth $25m. All this has now been redeemed for $8m payable in 2 years.

We have incorporated various firms - among them Purina, Lanera Austral, and the Bellavista Tome, Fiap, and the Fabrilana textile plants - into the area of public ownership - we have requisitioned the cement industry and the Yarur (textile) industry when supplies were threatened. In order to prevent bankruptcy, we have acquired an important share of the assets of the Zig Zag Publishing House, which forms a big part of our graphics and publishing industry, so that it can satisfy the social needs of the new Chile.

In all the firms that have been taken into public ownership, the nation can bear witness to the determined support of the workers, the immediate increase in productivity, and the active participation of workers, white- collar personnel and technicians in management and administration.

We have speeded up land reform and have already achieved a major part of this year's plan - the expropriation of one thousand big estates. The reform is going forward in accordance with existing legislation, and is protecting the interests of the small and medium-sized farmers. We want to build up a new and more vigorous agriculture, more solid in organization and more productive. We want the men who work the land to benefit fairly from the fruits of their labour. The state ownership of banks has been a decisive step. With absolute respect for the rights of the small shareholder, we have established state control over 9 banks and are on the point of obtaining majority control in the others. On the basis of previous experience, we are hoping for a reasonable settlement with foreign banks. We are thus trying to gain control of the financial apparatus and to widen the social area in the sectors which produce material goods. We want to place the new banking system at the service of the socialized area and of the small and medium-sized industrialists, merchants and farmers, who until now have been discriminated against.

Our present economic policy

These have been our first acts towards the initiation of the essential and definitive change in our economy. But we have done not only this. We have also planned a short-term policy whose central objective has been to increase the availability of material goods and services for consumption, and we have directed that increase towards the less favoured sectors.

We are carrying on a fierce struggle against inflation, and this is the key to our policy of redistribution. The fight against inflation has acquired a new political connotation - it will be a dynamic element in the popular struggle. To halt the rise in prices means that the people will maintain the increased spending power that has been given them, and this will be definitively consolidated with the deeper entrenchment of socialist organization. At the same time, independent businessmen can earn fair profits, the higher volume of production compensating for the smaller profits on each item.

In practice this policy has borne appreciable fruits in terms of redistribution. Nevertheless, we know that this planned reactivation faces obstacles. On the one hand, some groups of businesses are attempting to hinder the success of our measures by means of an open or a covert slowdown in production. On the other hand, some sectors which are imprisoned in a traditional model of low production and high profit lack audacity and are unable to understand the present juncture or to play a greater part in the productive process. To do so is, nevertheless, their social duty. To those who do not fulfil this duty, whether deliberately or not, we shall apply all the legal resources within our power to go on urging them and, if necessary, to make them produce more.

We are also carrying out a social policy to improve the diet of our children - to provide speedier medical care - to increase substantially the capacity of the educational system - to initiate the necessary housing construction programme - and to plan greater absorption of the unemployed as an urgent national need. We are doing this without disorder and with justice, endeavouring always to keep the social cost as low as possible. Today the citizen of our nation has greater buying power, consumes more and feels that the fruit of the common effort is better distributed. At the same time, he has the right to feel that he owns the mines, the banks, industry and the land, that he owns the future.

We are neither measuring ourselves against nor comparing ourselves with previous governments. We are fundamentally different. But if that comparison were to be made, using even the most traditional indicators, we would come out favourably. We have achieved the lowest rate of inflation in recent years - we have begun the most effective redistribution of revenues that Chile has ever seen. We shall build more houses this year than have ever been built before in a similar period. Despite the gloomy predictions, we have maintained the normal flow in supplies of essential goods.

Limits on Government action

We are fundamentally different from previous governments. This Government will always speak the truth to the people. I believe it is my duty to state honestly that we have committed mistakes - that unforeseen difficulties are slowing down the execution of plans and programs. But although the copper produced was not up to the target and although nitrate production did not reach a million tons, although we did not build all the houses that we planned, in each one of these sectors we have surpassed the highest rates that our country has ever recorded. We have not managed to coordinate adequately the various institutions of the State sector, owing to inefficiency in some decisions. But we are designing more expeditious methods of reationalizing and planning.

Immediately on assuming power, we set ourselves to fulfil our promises to the country. Together with the Central Workers' Federation we studied the Readjustments Law and signed the CWF-Government agreement. We have sent a bill to congress in which we propose for the public sector a pay rise 100% equal to the rise in the cost of living, and an increase on a greater scale in the corresponding minimum wages in the private sector. But I believe it was a mistake not to come to a broad agreement with the workers in order to arrive at more precise readjustments applicable in both the public and private sectors.

Another limitation that we have suffered lies in the administrative, legal and procedural deficiencies of some of the basic Government plans. For this reason the housing project, for example, got off to a slow start - and this has prevented the reactivation of certain industries and the absorption of a greater number of unemployed. In the months of April and May, economic activity connected with building began to get under way.

There is a vast area of public activity, comprising the public service sector, where there are deep-rooted evils. Millions of Chileans are the daily victims of bureaucratic paperwork, of delays and red tape. Each step requires dozens of transactions, forms, signatures and official stamps. How many hours are lost by every Chilean in his fight against red tape, how much creative energy is lost, how much useless irritation suffered. The Government authorities have still not directed sufficient effort towards eradicating this endemic evil. The most responsible sectors of white-collar workers have called attention to it.

We have also moved slowly in outlining the social machinery for the participation of the people. The bill which will give legal status to the CWF is now ready - it will institutionalized the participation of the workers in the political, social and economic management both of the state and of economic enterprises. But we have barely outlined the form their participation will take in the regions, in the communities and in private organizations. We ought to guarantee not only a vertical participation of workers in their separate branches - that of industrial workers, for example, in their plants - but also a horizontal participation which allows peasants, manufacturing workers, miners, white-collar workers and members of the professions to come together and discuss the problems of a particular economic region or of the country as a whole. These types of participation not only tend to bring about a fairer distribution of income but also help to ensure a greater yield.

This horizontal integration of the people is not easy and will doubtless require political maturity and collective consciousness, but it is well for us to start realizing now that the improvement of production on a collective farm depends also on workers in machinery and in tool and fertilizer plants, on the workers who build new roads, and on the small and medium-sized merchants who distribute the goods. Production is the responsibility of the working class as a whole.

Another criticism which we have to make of ourselves is that these first 6 months we have still not managed to mobilize the intellectual, artistic and professional capacity of many Chileans. There is some way to go before all scientists, members of the professional classes, builders, artists, technicians, householders, all those who can and wish to cooperate in the transformation of society, find a place in which they can use their talents.

Immediate tasks

In the remaining months of 1971, copper will definitely come under Chilean ownership. On the efforts of the workers, white-collar personnel and technicians of the Chuquicamata, El Teniente, Exotica, El Salvador and Andina mines depends to a great extent the volume of production which we shall achieve this year, and therefore our ability to obtain foreign exchange and so maintain normal supplies and realize our investment programmes. Copper represents the livelihood of Chile. Those who administer this wealth and those who extract it from the earth hold in their hands not only their own destiny and their own well-being but also the destiny and well-being of all Chileans.

We must extend land reform and if necessary modify the law, for if copper is Chile's livelihood, the land is its bread.

The land must be made to produce more. This is the responsibility of the peasants and of the small and medium-sized landowners, but the Government recognizes its mistakes and it is fair that others should also recognize theirs. The occupation of land by squatters, the indiscriminate occupation of agricultural terrains, are unnecessary and harmful. Belief in the Government is warranted by what we have done and by our attitudes. For this reason, the plans made by the Government and the time fixed for their execution must be respected. We invite political groups and individuals who are not in the Popular Unity to meditate seriously upon this.

The creation of the area of social ownership is one of our great objectives. The incorporation into this area of the major part of our basic wealth, the banks, the big estates and a large proportion of our foreign trade as well as of industrial and distributive monopolies is a task that we have already begun and that must now be amplified.

On the economic plane, the establishment of socialism means replacing the capitalist mode of production by a qualitative change in the relations of ownership - it also implies a redefinition of the relations of production. In this context, the creation of the area of social ownership has a human, political and economic significance. The incorporation of large sectors of the productive apparatus into a system of collective ownership puts an end to the exploitation of the worker, creates a deep feeling of solidarity, and permits the individual worker and his efforts to form part of the common work and the common endeavour.

In the political field, the working class knows that it is fighting for the socialization of our principle means of production. There is no socialism without an area of social ownership. To incorporate new firms day by day requires a permanent state of vigilance on the part of the working class. It also requires a high degree of responsibility. To construct socialism is not an easy task - it is not a short task. It is a long and difficult task in which the working class ought to participate in a disciplined, organized and politically responsible manner, avoiding anarchistic decisions and inconsistent voluntarism.

The importance of the public sector is traditional in our country. Approximately 40% of spending is public. More than 70% of investment is of State origin. The public sector was created by the national bourgeoisie in order to promote private accumulation and to consolidate the means of production, concentrating their technological resources and ownership.

Our government wants to make this sector quantitatively more important, but also to make it qualitatively different.

The State apparatus has been used by monopolies for the purpose of relieving their financial difficulties, for obtaining economic help and for strengthening the system. Up to now the public sector has been characterised by its subsidiary role in relation to the private sector. For this reason some public enterprises show large total deficits, while others are unable to produce profits comparable in size to those of some private enterprises.

Besides, the state machinery of Chile has lacked the necessary coordination between its different activities. As long as this is the case, it will be impossible for it to make a decisive contribution to a socialist economy. The control of some branches of production does not mean that the public sector has the machinery to direct and fulfil the objectives of socialism with respect to employment, saving, increase in productivity and the redistribution of income.

It is therefore necessary to widen the scope of public ownership and give it a new outlook. The expropriation of the most important means of production will permit the attainment of the degree of cohesion in this public machinery indispensable for the realization of the great national objectives. Hence one of the general criteria for the definition of the area of public ownership is the need to conceive this as a single, integrated whole, able to realise all its potentialities in a short or medium term.

This implies an urgent need to set up a planning system which devotes the economic surplus to the different productive assignments. This year we have begun to set up such a system, creating advisory bodies such as the National and Regional Development Councils. The Annual Plan for 1971 has been laid down and for the rest of the year, the planning organizations will work out the national economic plan for 1971-76. It is our intention that no investment project shall be carried forward unless it is included in these centrally approved Government plans. In this manner, we shall put an end to improvisation and begin to organize socialist planning in agreement with the Popular Unity programme. The existence of socialized ownership requires, by definition, a planning method which is both capable and effective and which is endowed with sufficient institutional power.

The advantages of socialism are not spectacularly displayed in the first stages of construction. But the creation of a real morality of work and the political mobilization of the proletariat not only around the government but also around the means of production will overcome the obstacles.

The establishment of the area of public ownership does not mean the creation of a State capitalism, but the true beginning of a socialist structure. The sector of public ownership will be directed jointly by the workers and by representatives of the State, as the uniting link between each enterprise and the whole of the national economy. It will not be inefficient bureaucratic enterprises but highly productive units which will lead the country's development and confer a new dimension on labour relations.

Our transitional regime does not consider the existence of the market as the only regulator of the economic process. Planning will be the main guide for the productive processes. Some will believe that there are other ways. But the formation of workers' enterprises integrated into the liberal market would mean dressing up wage-earners as so-called capitalists and pursuing a method which is a historical failure.

The supremacy of social ownership implies holding back and utilising the surplus that has been produced. It is therefore necessary to guarantee that the financial sector and a large part of the distributive sector be included in the area of public ownership. In short, we have to control the productive and financial processes and also, to some extent, the trade sector.

We have to strengthen the area of social ownership, pouring the power of the State, expressed in its economic policy, into this task - our credit policy, our fiscal, monetary and wage policies, our scientific and technological policies, our trade policy, must all be subordinated to the needs of socialist accumulation, that is to say, the interests of the workers.

Simultaneously, we must help the small and medium-sized industrialists, shopkeepers and farmers, who have for many years belonged to a sector exploited by the big monopolies, to make their contribution. Our economic policy guarantees them a fair deal. There will be no more financial exploitation, and the large-scale buyer's extortion from those who sell on a small scale will end. The small and medium-sized industries will play an active part in the new economy. Within a more rationally organized machinery which is directed towards production for the great majority of the nation, they will appreciate the support of the public sector. The limits of the private, mixed and public sectors will be precisely drawn.

We are facing an option for change unique in economic history. No country has achieved an acceptable economic development without huge sacrifices. We do not pretend to have discovered the recipe for making economic progress and achieving a fairer social system without cost. We are not offering to build overnight a socialized economy with fair distribution of income, with monetary stability and full employment, with high levels of productivity. On the other hand, we are offering to build that society at the least possible social cost imaginable in our circumstances. Socialism is not a free gift which people happen to find in their path. Neither is the liberation that accompanies it. Attaining it means postponing some present possibilities in exchange for founding a more humane, richer and more just society for the future.

Our foreign policy

The same principles which inform our internal policy inform the foreign policy of the country. In agreement with the United Nations Charter, our country resolutely supports non-intervention in the internal affairs of nations, juridical equality between them, and respect for their sovereignty and for the exercise of their right to self-determination.

My Government's foreign policy is directed both bilaterally and multilaterally towards the consolidation of peace and towards international cooperation. As a result, Chile has extended its diplomatic relations to new countries. Our first decision, in obedience to the wish of the majority of Chilean people, was to re-establish relations with Cuba, upon which unjust sanctions have been imposed. We have also established diplomatic and economic relations with China, Nigeria, and the German Democratic Republic. We have established commercial relations with the Democratic Republics of Korea and North Vietnam, and within the Latin American sphere we have supported the reduction of arms before the Organization of American States.

Chile collaborated in the Declaration of the Principles of International Law for Friendship and Cooperation Between Nations, adopted by the General Assembly of the United Nations at the end of last year. We have also supported a programme of action to apply the Declaration on the Granting of Independence to Colonial Nations and Peoples, and we have taken part in the formulation of the international strategy for the Second Decade of the United Nations Development Programme.

Our fight against under-development and against dependence on foreign hegemonies gives Chile a community of interests with the peoples of Africa and Asia. For this reason the Popular Government has decided to participate actively in the group of so-called unaligned nations and to take a determined part in their deliberations and agreements. Our concept of the universal scope of the United Nations leads us to vote in favour of the legitimate rights of the Chinese People's Republic. Our respect for the independence of all countries requires us to condemn the Vietnam war and its extension into Laos and Cambodia.

Within the general lines of this policy, we are collaborating in the United Nations Commission for Trade and Development (UNCTAD), the 3rd World conference of which will take place in Santiago in April 1972. Furthermore, I have the honour to inform you that I have received repeated invitations to visit countries of this and other continents. I have thanked these nations for their courtesy in the name of Chile.

It is the purpose of this Government to maintain friendly and cooperative relations with the United States. We have persevered in creating the conditions for making our position understood in order to avoid the outbreak of conflict and to prevent inessential questions from hindering this purpose and making it difficult to negotiate the friendly settlement of any problems that might arise. We believe that this realistic and objective course of action will be respected by the people and Government of the United States.

We have raised our voice as a sovereign people respected by all nations, and with the dignity of those who speak in the name of a worthy country. This we have done in the Economic Commission for Latin America (ECLA) and the Inter-American Committee for the Alliance for Progress (CIAP), and in all the special meetings where our representatives have expressed our thinking.

We have spoken repeatedly of the deep crisis which the inter-American system and its representative body, the Organization of American States (OAS), are passing through. The said system is based upon a supposed equality among its members when in fact there is absolute inequality, when the marked imbalance in favour of the United States protects the interests of the most powerful and prejudices those of the weaker nations. This takes place in a global context of dependence whose negative effects are evident at all levels. Thus the present dollar crisis, which had its origin in the internal and foreign policy of the United States, threatens to injure all the industrial capitalist countries. But it will have even more harmful repercussions upon the Latin American economies to the extent that it reduces our monetary reserves, diminishes our credit and restricts trade relations.

We also insist that the multilateral character of international financial organizations must be maintained free of all political pressures.

The member countries of these institutions cannot have their rights questioned because of the form of government they have chosen. And the international financial organizations cannot act on behalf of powerful countries against the weak. To use direct or hidden pressure in order to hinder the financing of technically suitable projects is to alter the declared aims of these organizations and represents a perverse way of interfering in the internal affairs of those countries in defiance of their needs.

Our efforts to broaden and strengthen all kinds of relations with the countries of Western Europe have been greeted with definite interest on their part, an interest which has already had real results.

In the increase in exchange and collaboration with the socialist countries my Government sees a suitable method of protecting our interests and stimulating the economy, technology, science and culture as a means of serving the working class of the entire world.

Latin America is in an abject state which none of its countries have been able to change by the traditional and ineffective means.

For some time, Colombia, Peru, Bolivia, Ecuador and Chile have proposed replacing the old formulas by new ones which, through regional integration, will permit the harmonious development of our resources in favour of our common objectives. The Andean Pact (signed in 1969) is an exemplary undertaking into which the Popular Unity Government is putting in all its efforts. We have demonstrated as much both in Lima and Bogota.

My Government attaches special importance to maintaining the best possible relations with the sister nations of the continent. It is our fundamental aim to strengthen all the links which will increase our continued friendship with the Argentine Republic, eliminating the obstacles which stand in the way of realising this objective. The anomalous state of our relations with the republic of Bolivia conflicts with the aims of both peoples, and for this reason we shall do everything in our power to restore them to normal.

The leading role of the workers

Everything we have discussed in the political, economic, cultural, and international fields represents the task of a whole nation, not that of one man or one government.

Between the months of November and February, the number of workers who have been obliged to go on strike has decreased from 170000 to 76000. The Popular Government's identification with the workers who share its successes and setbacks has made disputes unnecessary which were formerly inevitable. This year there have been no strikes in the coal, nitrate, copper, iron and textiles industries, the health services, education or railroads. In other words, there have been no strikes in those sectors which are vital to the nation's progress.

I should like to emphasise that for the first time in Chile, voluntary work has been introduced on a permanent basis in some state enterprises. And also, that for the first time it is being carried on in all areas of national life and on a massive scale from Arica to the Straits of Magellan. Soldiers, priests, students, workers, members of the professions and shopkeepers, old and young, are participating freely, spontaneously and in their own time in the common tasks. It is a much more creative development than working for profit. And it is an eloquent reply to those who, inside and outside Chile, would like to believe things that have never happened and never will. In this country there is and there will be a government which knows what methods to apply and when to apply them. As President, I assume responsibility for this.

The great achievements that lie before us will depend on the responsible and determined identification of the worker with his own real interests, which are more far-reaching than the small or big problems of this day, this month or this year. In the solidarity of the workers and their political representative, the Popular Government, we have an invincible instrument.

Those who live by their work have in their hands today the political direction of the State. It is a supreme responsibility. The building of the new social regime is based on the people, who are its protagonist and its judge. It is up to the State to guide, organize, and direct, but never to replace the will of the workers. In the economic as well as in the political field, the workers must retain the right to decide. To attain this means the triumph of the Revolution.

The people are fighting for this goal. They are fighting with the legitimacy that comes from respecting democratic values - with the assurance given by our programme - with the strength of being the majority - with the passion of the revolutionary.

We shall overcome.

Salvador Allende 1970

Chile: The First Battle

The electoral victory of People's Unity in Chile represents, for the first time, the ascent to power of a Latin-American people by way of the voting booth.

Never before in the republican history of the countries of Latin America has a true representative of the dispossessed classes, elected by the force of votes, directed the historic destiny of one of the nations that make up the geographic region in which the neocolonialist policy of world imperialism was born.

Since the beginning of the last century, the "divine" arrogance of the North American governors has been channeled according to the racist principle of "manifest destiny" and the interventionist policy of the Monroe Doctrine, to impose their neocolonial domination on the relations of capitalist production in Latin America.

The displacement of free market capitalism by monopolistic capitalism signified the beginning of the "era of exploitation" of the Latin-American economy by the Yankee monopolies that brought with them the conversion of the Hispanic republics into sources of raw materials for the industry of the metropolis and into profitable markets for Wall Street trade.

The economic control by the United States plutocracy over the fundamental means of production opened the doors to imperialist ideological penetration into the political scenario of lands located south of the Rio Grande, which have been "misgoverned" by their native oligarchies, faithful servants of the dollar empire that scatters the crumbs of the imperialist booty within the framework of the "inter-American system."

The triumph of the Cuban Revolution marked the beginning of the end of imperialist hegemony on this continent of underdevelopment, convulsed by hunger, misery and the death of millions of blacks, Indians and mestizos.

The presidential election of the socialist senator Salvador Allende is one of the historic events that advances the process of the second and definitive independence of the America of Bolivar, Marti and Che.

The new Chilean president has had to confront the maneuvers of the ruling classes that are not resigned to let go of the reins of power, and try to provoke economic chaos, incite the constitutional army to a military coup, and stir up reactionary terrorism against the political personalities of People's Unity.

In a speech made on October 11 at the plenary session of the Central Committee of the Socialist Party, which Tricontinental publishes in its entirety, the elected head of Araucanian land points out the historic mission of the People's Unity government, which will be to put into practice an economic policy to rescue the wealth of the country from foreign exploitation and eliminate the class inequality in Chile's social structure.

A few days before he was installed in the Moneda Palace, the socialist leader, who had the support of various progressive and left parties and movements in the electoral campaign for first magistrate of the nation, issued a call to the Chilean people to remain alert and vigilant in order to defend their political victory.

Dear Socialist comrades of Chile and Santiago,

Esteemed companion and friend, Secretary-General of the Socialist Party, Senator Aniceto Rcdriguez, Comrade leaders of the Central

Committee and of the regional committees of the country,

Very dear and esteemed friends and national leaders of the parties and movements that comprise People's Unity,

Socialist members of Parliament and people's members of Parliament, socialist governors and mayors, Members of People's Unity:

It is a very moving and profound event for me to raise my voice in a Party meeting ending hours of work and our collective preoccupation for the future of Chile and its working masses.

For me — you must understand this well — it is a feeling of intimate, profound and strong emotion to be here speaking to you as a socialist, because I will never forget that what I am, have been and will be I owe to the Party, to the people, to the understanding of FRAP (People's Action Front) yesterday, and today to People's Unity — I tell you comrades — talking to you has a profound significance for me because the years that I have lived within this, the socialist family, crowd together in my memory.

Founder of the Party in Valparaiso and participating member of its first central committees, within Party life, in an expression of internal democracy, I have held all positions including — on two occasions — Secretary-

General of our collectivity and deputy, minister, senator and today socialist President through the will of the people.

My friend Senator Volodia Teitelboim has done very well speaking in the name of the parties and the People's Unity movement, and Aniceto Rodriguez in recalling our fallen comrades — I wish also this morning to recall the old-timers and render homage to a worker who has been incorporated into the Party since its birth, leader of the bakers, who has been ill for years but is here today, to say that he and his class know that this is their victory.

I render homage to the workers in the person of Isidoro Godoy, leader of the bakers.

I wish to point out, and I know that in doing so I touch a sister of ours very deeply, I wish to recall one who was the best of the best, the Secretary-General of the Party, the Senator who fell organizing the Chilean peasants. I wish to render homage to all those who have fallen, in the ever-present name of our comrade, Salomén Corbalan.

Comrades, we socialists come together after a victory which is ours but not only ours. And the Party must understand this very thoroughly and I must insist on it very strongly.

The victory that has been won is not the victory of a man; the victory that has been won is not the victory of the Socialist Party. The victory won, the victory achieved, is the victory of People's Unity, it is Chile's victory.

The Party has a greater responsibility, and I know that it is going to meet that responsibility because after November 4 a member from its ranks will be President. Moreover, each Party member, its old members, its adults, its generous and sacrificing women, its tough youngsters of the Socialist Youth Federation, must understand that this is an extraordinary responsibility. That, as Aniceto Rodriguez has said, it goes beyond the frontiers of the nation. That there is a responsibility in the common victory of the People's Unity. This responsibility must grow in each member of our collective.

We must be the most united, we must be the most sacrificing, we must be the example in the fulfillment of duties, we must show an unshakable morality; in summary, we must be socialists in the service of the people and in the service of the Chilean revolution.

Only thus, only thus can we answer the confidence given us by other parties and movements that are a part of the People's Unity. They also had the right to have one of their members carry the banner of the people. They had the responsibility, sufficient breadth and democratic practice to place this banner, which is the hope of the fatherland, in the hands of one of your men. Because of this the socialists must understand the supreme responsibility implied in having triumphed and in having the fundamental base of this victory in one of your men who has contributed to the formation of a consciousness throughout Chile in his 37 years of life within the Socialist Party.

Comrades, this being my thought as I stand here before you, I wish to single out some recent political events. Before the Party now, and tomorrow always before the people, I will tell you, in the form of a fraternal and responsible dialogue, all that is happening in this country and the projections our action as governor can achieve in the international field.

I wish to say that the meeting of the 4th of September ended following exemplary and extraordinary behavior by the people of Santiago and the people of Chile — yes, because 200000 or more people assembled the night of the 4th from Arica to Magallanes, from the mountains to the sea, and thousands and thousands of men and women of the people also gaily celebrated their victory, their own victory, which is also our victory — and we did so with a lofty feeling of patriotism, and we did it with an exemplary attitude, and we did it without arrogance, we did it, more than anything else, with responsibility.

And this is what will give the people the strength to be able to say as well that we had this attitude, that we did not and will not cease to have it, because if the legal channels seem fully opened, there are still the obstinate who are trying to prevent our victory. But let them be aware that this serenity is not to disarm the people, that this tranquility is the tranquility of those who are strong, it is the firmness of those who know how and when they must proceed.

With a people like the people of Chile, it is very difficult, it is impossible that on the 4th of November the people should not enter the governor's house with me.

The steps we have taken publicly, meaning, as comrade and friend Aniceto Rodriguez said, that People's Unity, with the people, has conversed with the Christian Democrats in order to convert into Constitutional amendments, ideas that were in our program. I say that this dialogue took place with the people's knowledge and that no one in Chile can deny that our acceptance of an attitude that we consider to be just does not imply, nor can it imply in any way, a modification in the content of the program People's Unity puts forth.

And it is honest and it is just that the people understand that within Christian Democracy itself there were sectors that were in opposition.

But there was a majority that understood that they also had a responsibility to the people, not only because of its majority composition as a social force among the workers, but also because of the proposals formulated in the face of Chile's conscience by their candidate Senor Tomic. And this afternoon I expressed my recognition of the attitude and the political honesty of Radomiro Tomic and of the attitude taken by the leader of Christian Democracy, Senator Benjamin Prado.

But by the same token and reaffirming what Aniceto Rodriguez has said, I respectfully [exclamations from the people] — quiet comrades - and very clearly ask the Chief of State not to rush through Congress certain laws that do not have a clear explanation, just as he obtained President Alessandri's agreement, for example, to postpone the beginning of work on Lo Prado tunnel, to resolve it finally under Frei's governorship.

From this tribune I ask him that the project on national television not be speeded up.

I ask President Frei not to insist on the veto which implies not just nonremoval of functionaries, whose careers we are going to respect, but a limitation on the possibility of placing our own people in the vital administrative and economic centers, It is not a question of a struggle for bureaucratic posts but that the levers of the economy must be in the hands of those who are going to govern the country.

I respectfully but clearly request President Frei not to accelerate the creation of the Metropolitan Association because it is an investment in a project that the People's Unity government must determine.

I request of President Frei that his Minister of Mines not speed up an association of mixed capital between a socialist country and Chile. This problem must be resolved by the future government, by my government, by the people's government.

The country — Aniceto Rodriguez noted it and also Volodia Teitelboim pointed it out in greater summary — has lived through a stage, I should say, the last or next to last death rattle of the ultrareactionary right. The economic panic, the economic chaos it has tried to unleash, the illicit and cunning commerce with foreign exchange and money in order to prejudice the escudo, the failure to buy raw materials, the unnecessary sale of cattle, the difficulties in spring planting, all this underscored by one unwonted fact of Chilean political life: the direct attack on the common good endangering the life of innocent people.

How many times have we said it, how many times have we explained to the people that we would never resort to unnecessary violence nor to personal terrorism, that this is not a part of the tactics of the people.

We have seen how bombs and bombs and bombs have been placed in the face of the inefficiency of the investigatory services, and secondly in the face of an attitude on the part of Judicial Power toward these first arrested that I do not wish to analyze in depth.

I do want to say to the people that the investigatory agent who pointed out the presence of the Schillings and the Gonzalez who were first arrested, affirmed — and the pertinent authority knew of it — that from the car in which he was taken to be shown the locations where the bombs were going to be planted, they had told him that, from there they had fired on the humble guardsman who was in the service of the British Embassy.

I say to the people that we are not going to permit and will not tolerate dropping exhaustive investigations which would punish the law breakers. What would never occur is that a man of the left would attack a modest functionary. As they know, we are aware of who the culprits are and we want them to understand that we know their names, but that justice and the government of Frei have the obligation of revealing them now and not tomorrow.

Comrades, listen well to this: these seditious attitudes are not improvised. There are foreign advisers here, people with experience, mercenaries sent in to create this climate. That is where the responsibility is yours. Four hundred thousand and some votes we received in Santiago. I always said this is not just one more electoral battle. If we received 400000 and some votes, that makes 800000 eyes, 800000 ears that must be alert to tell the people of Chile and the present government who they are and where they come from.

Each one of you must meet this duty, which is not one of informing but rather is a patriotic duty to defend the country's welfare and to prevent the attempt to wrest the people's victory from them by cunning and cowardly means.

Comrades: a very small and impersonal chapter. I told you about it at the big meeting in the Alameda. The insolence of the reactionaries reached the point of saying that a general or admiral in the Chilean army or navy was worth 500000 dollars. I told the people: we have said and we reaffirm that we have confidence in the word of the Chilean soldier who treats our armed forces as forces that are professional and independent but responsible to the dictates of the law and the Constitution.

I know that the dignity of a Chilean soldier has no price in the market of international crime, If there are those who claim this they will meet with the answer of the people in uniform, the armed forces of the country.

For this reason — and also because they are businessmen — they said it is cheaper to eliminate Allende. Three hundred million pesos will do it.

In Valparaiso there is a Mr. Montero that I am going to tell you about, who belonged to one of the branches of the armed forces and who talked too much and said that on the 17th they are going to assassinate me in Valparaiso. I am going to Valparaiso on the 17th and Mr. Montero and his accomplices are not going to be able to accomplish their mission.

But if something should happen to me, let them understand that the people of Chile know perfectly well that I am only one of you, there is no one who is irreplaceable. And the highest homage that could be given a fallen comrade would be to continue fighting by every means possible to win the revolution and victory.

In addition to this aspect of internal policy, I have an obligation to inform the people very briefly on certain events of international importance.

It has been said that we would invite such and such persons and that we would not invite others. At the moment and in accord with custom it is the Frei government that handles official invitations. We will handle ours through the Central Workers' Union, the Youth Command of People's Unity and the universities.

I also have the right to invite certain personalities and I say that we will invite whomever we consider it convenient to invite without submitting to any authority other than our own the right to invite whomever we please.

I have already pointed out that your victory, the people's victory, has brought forth an incalculable degree of solidarity. Thousands and thousands of cables have come from all parts of the world, letters and communications from all progressive, revolutionary and authentically democratic forces. I can tell you that I have already been invited by the socialists of Sweden and of Norway, for example, that I have been invited by the Italian socialists, that I have been invited by peoples' movements in Latin America.

I want to single out as an example the letter received — and it is a shame there isn't time for me to read it — from the former President of Mexico, whose name is engraved in the consciousness of the men of Latin America. I refer to the man who nationalized oil and began the march toward agrarian reform for the commoners, the general and the man always present in the people's struggle, Lazaro Cardenas.

Official information emanating from the organizations responsible permits me to tell you that from July to September 5300 North American citizens have entered the country.

Welcome tourists, welcome journalists, intellectuals, artists, North American citizens who are authentically North Americans, and are therefore representatives of the people who understand our right, which is irrenounceable.

And unwelcome! Because among these 5300 a not insignificant percentage of CIA agents must have infiltrated. Let them understand that we are vigilant and that if Chile's frontiers are open in a fraternal fashion to those clean and responsible citizens of any country, the fist of Chile, of its people, of People's Unity, will fall implacably on those who try to alter our lives by the criminal methods of international traffic.

Thirty Cuban gusanos have arrived. We know their names and we're just about able to say that we know where they are hiding. From that point on, we advise the investigation authority — and I personally advised the director of investigations yesterday — that we will take no individual action. Until November 3, this government is responsible. Let it fulfill its duty. But let it know that we are alert, and those who have been traitors to their country, their revolution and their blood are not going to come here to sow counterrevolution. If they were thrown out or left their country, they will also leave here punished.

I am hurt and concerned, because I have respect for the dignity of the position, that the President of the Congress of Chile, Senator Tomas Pablo [exclamations from the people] — silence, comrades — has said that 40 or more Hungarians have entered Chile, that they came to train the guerrillas. I believe Senator Tomas Pablo is a little behind the times.

What happened is that, for the first time in 1969, the famous great spectacular of Budapest came — the Hungarian state circus.

That is what Senator Tomas Pablo must be referring to.

As for the other Hungarians, it is regrettable that he told the country his information was authentic because it had been given to him by a Minister of State.

Well, regrettably for the President of the Congress of Chile, head of one of the state powers, his statements have been demolished by the Hungarian representative in Chile, and also by a letter published in all the daily newspapers by the Hungarian Chargé d'Affaires in Chile and even by the Chilean Ministry of Foreign Affairs itself.

The Chargé d'Affaires or the Hungarian Ambassador in Chile told the President of the Chilean Senate that actually guerrillas had entered but that they are engaged in an educational guerrilla activity, that they are university professors, and that they have been in Chile for several years.

It is regrettable that the head of a public office has to receive such a hard lesson from a representative of another country and from Chile's own representative in Hungary. And it is to be hoped that Mr. Tomas Pablo will never again forget this lesson.

A daily newspaper whose name I will not mention and which you know and know why I do not name it, has launched a steady attack against People's Unity in a series of editorials. But there is one editorial in this paper which in my judgment has an extraordinary intent and a deceitful point of view. Not only does it touch on aspects of national life but also projects its sinister imagination onto the international scene. And it maintains that Chile is going to be isolated, that we will not be able to trade with Latin-American countries, that we are going to be outside the international organizations.

Very well. This is what that editorial said when the press stated among other things that I had conversed for long hours with Felipe Herrera, president of the BID (Inter-American Developmental Bank). And if I conversed with him it is because I am interested in knowing what credits Chile has or can obtain.

That I had conversed with the ex-President of Colombia, Carlos Lleras Restrepo, with whom we analyzed the perspectives of the Andes Pact.

These journalists know that Pedro Zusjoric, under my direct charge, had conversed with the Argentine commercial representative to explain our problem concerning the desire to increase commercial interchange with Argentina, which I believe already comes to $200 000 000 a year.

Very well, they knew all this. And nevertheless they write an editorial stating that our proposal is to isolate Chile.

Here before all the people gathered in the Caupolican Theater, and to those who are listening over the whole network, I tell you: we are going to have diplomatic and commercial relations with all the countries of the world, only by defending Chile's interests and recognizing that commerce is bilateral and that there are reciprocal interests in buying and selling.

We will not give up any market, nor any trade. Not in Europe, nor the United States. But we have the right to effectively seek out new markets, and we will do so without asking anyone's permission, looking out for Chile's interests only. And we are going to stay in the OAS (Organization of American States) in order to expound our position within this somewhat unprestigious organization. We will go to the United Nations taking the ideas, the proposals and the creative sentiment of the people's government of Chile, and we will stimulate the LAFTA (Latin-American Free Trade Association) because this course is correct for the country, and we will stimulate the Andes Pact more and more in order to have more trade with Ecuador, with Peru, with Bolivia and with

Colombia, and hopefully Venezuela will join the Andes Pact.

It is true that we will have our criteria there, in the sense that this trade benefits the people and not the imperialist monopolies and national oligarchies.

And this is what we will do in the international field. But briefly — and I hope you hear me in silence because it is not a matter of making an agitational speech — I want to explain to the socialists and to Chile in brief form (and I am pleased that it is 2 pm, which proves to me that the people's spiritual hunger is greater than their material hunger), I am going to explain some essential ideas that we are going to carry out which must interest everyone here and all those listening.

In the economic field, we must start the People's Unity program going. We do not hide the magnitude of the task that we have proposed. We will receive an economy of the sharpened contradictions of a regime which at the very least has been incapable of resolving the people's essential problems.

The unemployment figures were already very high before September 4 and new problems of unemployment have been added in the last weeks. In addition to the low level of economic growth, the activities of important sectors have fallen still further. Inflationary pressures have been accentuated, resulting in a 33% increase in the cost of living in the current year. The fiscal situation has deteriorated. Because I can point out that according to the technical office of the United Nations, Chile is surpassed only by South Viet Nam in the inflationary process. The people know very well what is behind the maneuvers that have taken place in the last few weeks. You know that the big foreign monopolistic and national interests have moved with double finality to create a chaotic economic situation and to search for a way to ignore the people's will. Or at the least to create conditions that interfere as much as possible with our action after the 4th of November.

The workers know or should know very well that we have a job to do now in the face of these unpatriotic maneuvers. It is necessary to watch and to denounce anyone who fails to replace raw materials that have been stored, or who takes out and does not replace stocks of spare parts, is careless in maintaining machinery. It is necessary to watch and to denounce any maneuver directed against the criminal debilitation of the productive capacity.

I was in Concepcion. The comrades in the Bellavista cloth industry recited their tragedy to me and I said publicly that if we could not personally resolve it, because we were not the government, we could raise our voice and our effort to solve this problem which had dragged on for three months or more. And when the Ready-To-Wear

Association came to talk to me, they explained that no one had been dismissed but that they lacked raw materials from Bellavista. I knew that the owner of this industry had gone to Buenos Aires. It seems that he received a message, returned, and because of the intervention of our people in the Ministry of Work, the problem was solved and the aforementioned empresario, in a trembling hand, signed what he had not wished to sign if three months. Not by imposition but because it was correct that he sign it. And so the workers of Bellavista are working again and those who are a part of the Ready-To-Wear Association are going to receive their raw materials.

Similarly I sent a letter to the Chuquicamata workers. The petition requests were not taken care of and a strike was called. I sent a communication to these workers to tell them to realize that, respecting their rights and without renouncing them, this strike must be resolved quickly, and let no worker think that we won't explain to him the meaning of the disproportionate rise that brings as its consequence — as in copper — a chain reaction not only in the copper market enterprise, but also in the inflationary national process.

When the moment for the readjustment of pay and salaries arrives, comrades, I will speak to the people, I will explain what scale we are going to use, and I know perfectly well that the people will support it. In our judgment, the Chuquicamata strike must start on the path to solution because we will not wish to receive a more damaged national economy, because the very enterprise that knows we are going to nationalize it will be able to behave generously at the last minute, at our expense; and while respecting the rights of the Chuquicamata workers, we are not going to create a workers' aristocracy in any work sector.

I am certain that the copper workers will understand this language. And they will understand that the government of the people is their government, and so they and the rest of the workers are not going to allow themselves to be pushed into strikes, and without renouncing their rights nor the irrevocable right to strike, they will find just and speedy solutions in order to defend, now above all, the national economy.

Therefore, I want the comrades who are listening to me to understand that the present difficulties cannot obscure our principal objectives. Our gigantic task is to master the conditions which the present system has been incapable of resolving.

Greater economic expansion and, at the same time, control of inflationary pressures. Rapid increase in productivity and at the same time greater use of the workforce. Greater speed in technological advancement and at the same time less dependency on sources from which the techniques come. Greater dovetailing of the Chilean economy with that of other Latin-American countries, as I already said, and at the same time full ability to differentiate our objectives for internal transformation. To that end we must undertake from the first day of government the basic changes outlined in the People's Unity program. The character of these changes will be reflected in two fundamental aspects: in the relationship of domination and control of the Chilean economy. Listen carefully: the essential point is the substitution of foreign domination and certain large monopolistic interests by social domination of an extent and type compatible with the continuation and development of private productive activities.

The categorical reply to what I am suggesting is contained in the program of the People's Unity in the three areas that this program covers. The area of social ownership: its conduct of the economy. In this there is no revenge nor zeal to expropriate simply to expropriate. Listen carefully, neither revenge nor zealous expropriation for expropriation's sake, in which we appear as pseudorevolutionaries. But by the same token we say that expropriation is necessary in order to develop the Chilean economy, that we are going to do it implacably without any type of bargaining.

In order to insure the operations and strengthen the social area of this economy, Chile's control of its basic wealth is indispensable: its copper, iron, steel. Public control of all financial mechanisms such as banks — let it be known — social ownerships of basic activities, strategic to the process of development, capable of generating a volume of surpluses whose channeling cannot be allowed to be surrendered to monopoly capital. Example: the iron and steel industry — that is to say, steel and its derivatives.

In the area of mixed industry there will have to be an integration by means of activities in which there is an interest in reconciling — let them note this — the means of assuring a social function, along with the private enterprises. For example, automobile assembly, certain lines of production of capital goods: agricultural machinery, for instance. Not only will state decisions contribute to the set up in these areas but we will also accept and seek the initiative of those private sectors that have a spirit of nationalism and understand what we wish to do and the means by which we are going to succeed.

The private sector: in this area there are 30000 or more small- and medium-sized industries or enterprises and crafts that we are going to aid.

Their perspectives are not those of subsistence but rather operation under better conditions than now exist, with more precise and stable regulations within the framework of a plan of national economic development which is not subject to the whims of the big monopolies, on whom they now depend for raw material supplies, distribution of their products, etc.

With easier credit terms, less bureaucratic control and the important simplification of the system imposed. What is important in defining the extension of each area is a fundamental criteria: that the basic decisions concerning the future of the national economy do not depend on interests that are tied up with foreign capital and certain national monopolistic groups, but rather on the legitimate interests of Chile and her people. For this reason, we have said that the program of People's Unity breaks Chile's economic dependency, breaks Chile's political dependency, and breaks Chile's cultural dependency. We want to be a free country economically and sovereign master of its social and political destiny, comrades.

Consequently, all these measures will be taken to reorient the productive force toward the necessities of the great masses of the population. The distribution of profits will be different so that the extremes of wealth and poverty will be eradicated, As I have told you, we cannot tolerate the fact that, as far as pensions are concerned, for example, 80% of the workers receive 247 escudos a month while there are rich men who receive 20 or 25 million pesos' in monthly pensions. This is going to be ended — definitively, comrades.

We must raise the levels of popular consumption, control squandering and waste in the form of lavish consumer goods. The structure of the productive capacity will have to be adjusted to this change in distribution of revenues, The task of reorientation is enormous in taxes, in the traditional attitude of enterprise. In the new method that has to be developed, in the reconversion of what now exists there is a true challenge for the technicians and the industrialists themselves. Essential consumer products must be guaranteed. Large segments of the population must be raised to higher levels of consumption and forms of human existence. We cannot tolerate the moral and physiological misery in which millions of Chileans live. Our battle is against hunger, against unemployment, against the lack of housing and education. And we are going to conquer as we have conquered and will conquer and overthrow exploitation and misery.

For the first time in history we will be able to evaluate for purposes of our own interests, the natural resources in which we are extraordinarily rich. Our task is to be capable of projecting ourselves onto the world market as great and efficient producers of copper goods and not only as important exporters of raw copper. The same is true of our forest reserves and other activities.

In sum, a reorientation that raises us to the level of efficient producers of popular consumer goods. To sustain this production with our own capacity for making possible new equipment and the necessary basic investments. For specialization in several central industrial lines on a high technological level which will allow us to enter the world market without complexes.

This is our task in the economic field for these first years. And as time is short I want to reiterate and affirm only that this is the initial stage we must reach, after which will indisputably come the six-year plans that we are going to fulfill year after year and in which the people will participate not only by understanding but also by discussion.

And here too, socialist comrades, women and men, I want you to understand definitely that everything must be viewed with a new mentality. Yesterday we were the fighting opposition against the regime and the system.

From the 4th on, we will be the government and, comrades, then we are going to have to measure not only our responsibility but pour out our creative capacity as well. And while singing our revolutionary hymn which we hold so close to our socialist hearts, I say to you: perhaps we must sing these verses for the last time. Do not forget that there is a stanza which says: "against the present shame." After November 4 we're not going to be able to say that, comrades [laughter from the people]. I say that because I am sure that we are capable of fulfilling our goals.

And this is the task, among others, of the Party: to be ever vigilant, pushing, pushing, and pushing ahead, comrades, toward the achievement of the true liberation of Chile and of its heritage.

You already have a vision then, however small. of the aspects we wish to confront. of the national and international projections of the people's government.

I have already said here. and it must be emphasized, that this is the first time in the history of the world that a people has won the government by electoral means in order to take power from the government and use the power to make revolutionary changes which permit the creation of a new society, a new morality. a new life and a new concept of man and of the human couple.

We are undertaking an extraordinary task and one made more difficult by the vacillations of the government of Mr. Frei since the 4th of September, with an insolent, provocative, conspiratorial attitude or the part of reactionary sectors in Chile that have wished to waste the national economy and destroy without concern for the harm it does to Chile, goods that belong to everyone, and endangering the lives of innocent human beings.

How well the people have already learned what it means to talk of democracy and not practice it! How well the people have already learned the lesson that those who talk about respecting all victories meet the victory of the people by trying to close the roads and even reach the point of using foreign mercenaries to prevent our triumph!

But comrades, finally and now I say to you socialists gathered in this theater and to those who are listening to me throughout the country that, with the profound satisfaction of being a founding member of the Party and with the awareness that I am also a founder of People's Unity, I will come to the government knowing that the people will always stimulate me to move forward, that the people, with legitimate right, will demand explanations if by chance I should hesitate.

But that the people must know, and on this I stake my word as a social fighter, that never will they see me retreat, and I cannot retreat because you are the barricades that say Chile has the right to advance and advance until it is possible for the man and the woman of our nation to have a new life, to make a different kind of nation a possibility, with its own characteristics, so that Chile is a family from Arica to Magallanes and from the mountains to the sea, because we are a people united in the great national task of making possible the material and spiritual progress of Chileans.

Comrades, we won yesterday, we will win today and we will win tomorrow because we remain united and because, comrades, we are the people.

Salvador Allende

Speech to the United Nations (excerpts)

4 December 1972

I come from Chile, a small country but one where today any citizen is free to express himself as he so desires. A country of unlimited cultural, religious and ideological tolerance and where there is no room for racial discrimination. A country with its working class united in a single trade union organization, where universal and secret sufrage is the vehicle of determination of a multiparty regime, with a Parliament that has been operating constantly since it was created 160 years ago; where the courts of justice are independent of the executive and where the constitution has only been changed once since 1833, and has almost always been in effect. A country where public life is organized in civilian institutions and where the armed forces are of a proven professional background and deep democratic spirit. A country with a population of almost 10,000,000 people that in one generation has had two first-place Nobel Prize winners in literature, Gabriela Mistral and

Pablo Neruda, both children of simple workers. In my country, history, land and man are united in a great national feeling.

But Chile is also a country whose retarded economy has been subjected and even alienated to foreign capitalists firms, resulting in a foreign debt of more than US$ 4,000 million whose yearly services represent more than 30 per cent of the value of the country's exports; whose economy is extremely sensitive to the external situation, suffering from chronic stagnation and inflation; and where millions of people have been forced to live amidst conditions of exploitation and misery, of open or concealed unemployment.

Today I have come because my country is confronting problems of universal significance that are the object of the permanent attention of this assembly of nations: the struggle for social liberation, the effort for well-being and intellectual progress and the defence of national identity and dignity.

The outlook which faced my country, just like many other countries of the Third World, was a model of reflex modernization, which, as technical studies and the most tragic realities demonstrate, excludes from the possibilities of progress, well being and social liberation more and more millions of people, destining them to a subhuman life. It is a model that will produce a greater shortage of housing, that will condemn an ever-greater number of citizens to unemployment, illiteracy, ignorance and physiological misery.

In short, the same perspective that has kept us in a relationship of colonization or dependency and exploitation in times of cold war, has also operated in times of military conflict or in times of peace. There is an attempt to condemn us, the underdeveloped countries, to being second-class realities, always subordinated.

This is the model that the Chilean working class, coming on the scene as protagonist of its own destiny, has decided to reject, searching in turn for a speedy, autonomous development of its own, and transforming the traditional structures in a revolutionary manner.

The people of Chile have won the Government after a long road of generous sacrifices, and it is fully involved in the task of installing economic democracy so that productive activity will operate in response to needs and social expectations and not in the interests of individual profit. In a programmed and coherent manner, the old structure, based on the exploitation of the workers and the domination of the main means of production by a minority, is being overcome. It is being replaced by a new structure -led by the workers and placed at the service of the interests of the majority- which is laying the foundations for a growth that will represent real development, that will include all the population and not cast aside vast sectors of the people and doom them to poverty and to being social outcasts. The workers are driving the privileged sectors from political and economic power, both in the centres of labour as well as in the communes and in the state. This is the revolutionary content of the process my country is going through for overcoming the capitalist system and opening the way for a socialist one.

The need to place all our economic resources at the service of the enormous needs of the people went hand in hand with Chile's regaining of its dignity. We had to end the situation as a result of which we Chileans, plagued by poverty and stagnation, had to export huge sums of capital for the benefit of the world's most powerful market economy. The nationalization of basic resources constitutes an historic demand. Our economy could no longer tolerate the subordination implied by having more than 80 per cent of its exports in the hands of a small group of large foreign companies that have always put their interests before those of the countries in which they make profits. Neither could we accept the curse of the latifundium, the industrial and trade monopolies, credit for just a few and brutal inequality in the distribution of income.

THE REVOLUTIONARY PATH THAT CHILE IS FOLLOWING

The change in the power structure that we are carrying out, the progressive leadership role of the workers in it, the national recovery of basic riches, the liberation of our country from subordination to foreign powers, are all crowning points of a long historical process; of efforts to impose political and social freedoms, of heroic struggle of several generations of workers and farmers to organize themselves as a social force to obtain political power and drive the capitalists from economic power.

Its tradition, personality and revolutionary awareness make it possible for the Chilean people to give a boost to the process towards socialism, strengthening civic liberties, collective and individual, and respecting cultural and ideological pluralism. Ours is a permanent battle to install social freedoms and economic democracy through full exercise of political freedoms.

The democratic will of our people has taken upon itself the challenge of giving a boost to the revolutionary process in the framework of a highly institutionalized state of law, that has been flexible to changes and is today faced by the need to adjust to the new socio- economic reality.

We have nationalized basic riches, we have nationalized copper, we have done so by a unanimous decision of Parliament, where the government parties are in a minority. We want everyone to clearly understand that we have not confiscated the large foreign copper mining firms. In keeping with constitutional provisions, we have righted a historic injustice by deducting from the compensation all profits above 12 per cent a year that they had made since 1955.

Some of the nationalized firms had made such huge profits in the last 15 years that when 12 per cent a year was applied as the limit of reasonable profits, they were affected by important deductions. Such is the case, for example, of a branch of the Anaconda Company, which made profits in Chile of 21.5 per cent a year over its book value between 1955 and 1970, while Anaconda's profits in other countries were only 3.6 per cent a year. That is the situation of a branch of the Kennecott Copper Corporation, which in the same period of time, made an average of 52.8 per cent profits a year in Chile -and in some years it made really incredible profits like 106 per cent in 1967, 113 per cent in 1968 and more than 205 per cent in 1969. In the same period of time, Kennecott was making less than 10 per cent a year in profits in other countries. However, the application of the constitutional norm has kept other copper firms from suffering deductions because their profits did not exceed the reasonable limit of 12 per cent a year.

We should point out that in the years just before the nationalization, the large copper firms had started expansion plans, which have failed in large measure and to which they did not contribute their own resources, in spite of the huge profits they made, and which they financed through foreign credits. In keeping with legal ruling, the Chilean state must take charge of these debts that reach the enormous figure of more than US$ 727 million. We have even started to pay debts that one of those firms had with Kennecott, its parent company in the United States.

These same firms that exploited Chilean copper for many years made more than US$ 4,000 million in profits in the last 42 years alone, while their initial investments were less than US$ 30 million. A simple and painful example, an acute contrast: in my country there are 600,000 children who can never enjoy life in normally human terms, because in the first eight months of their existence they did not receive the elementary amount of proteins. My country, Chile, would have been totally transformed by these US$ 4,000 million. Only a small part of this amount would assure proteins for all the children in my country once and for all.

The nationalization of copper has been carried out while strictly observing internal judicial order and with respect for the norms of international law, which there is no reason to identify with the interests of the big capitalist firms.

In short, this is the process my country is going through, and I feel it is useful to present it to this assembly, with the authority given to us by the fact that we are strictly fulfilling the recommendations of the United Nations and relying on internal efforts as the base for economic and social development. Here, in this forum, the change of institutions and backward structures has been advised, along with the redistribution of income, priority for education and health and care for the poorest sectors. All this is a essential part of our policy and it is in the process of being carried out.

THE FINANCIAL BLOCKADE

That is why it is even more painful to have to come here to this rostrum to proclaim the fact that my country is the victim of grave aggression.

We had foreseen problems and foreign resistance to our carrying out our process of changes, especially in view of our nationalization of natural resources. Imperialism and its cruelty have a long and ominous history in Latin America and the dramatic and heroic experience of Cuba is still fresh. The same is the case with Peru, which has had to suffer the consequences of its decision to exercise sovereign control over its oil.

In the decade of the 70s, after so many agreements and resolutions of the international community, in which the sovereign right of every state to control its natural resources for the benefit of its people is recognized, after the adoption of international agreements on economic, social and cultural rights and the strategy of the second decade of development, which formalized those agreements, we are the victims of a new expression of imperialism -more subtle, more sneaky, and terribly effective- to block the exercise of our rights as a sovereign state.

From the very moment of our election victory on 4 September 1970, we were affected by the development oflarge-scale foreign pressures, aimed at blocking the inauguration of a government freely elected by the people and then overthrowing it. There have been efforts to isolate us from the world, strangle the economy and paralyze the sale of copper, our main export product, and keep us from access to sources of international financing.

We realize that when we denounce the financial-economic blockade with which we were attacked, it is hard for international public opinion and even for many of our compatriots to easily understand the situation because it is not open aggression, publicly proclaimed before the whole world. Quite the contrary, it is a sneaky and double-crossing attack, which is just as damaging to Chile.

We find ourselves opposed by forces that operate in the shadows, without a flag, with powerful weapons that are placed in a wide range of influential positions.

We are not the object of any trade ban. Nobody has said that he seeks a confrontation with our country. It would seem that our only enemies or opponents are the logical internal political ones. That is not the case. We are the victims of almost invisible actions, usually concealed with remarks and statements that pay lip service to respect for the sovereignty and dignity of our country. But we have first-hand knowledge of the great difference that there is between those statements and the specific actions we must endure.

I am not mentioning vague matters, I am discussing concrete problems that affect my people today and which will have even more serious economic repercussions in the coming months.

Chile, like most of the nations of the Third World, is very vulnerable to the situation of the external sector of its economy. In the last 12 months, the decline in the international price of copper has represented a loss of about US$ 200 million in income for a nation whose exports total a bit more than US$ 1,000 million, while the products, both industrial and agricultural, that we must import are much more expensive now, in some cases as much as 60 per cent.

As is almost always the case, Chile buys at high prices and sells at low prices.

It has been at these moments, in themselves difficult for our balance of payments, that we have had to face, among others, the following simultaneous actions, apparently designed to take revenge on the Chilean people for their decision to nationalize copper.

Until the moment my Government took office, every year Chile received almost US$ 80 million in loans from international financial organizations such as the World Bank and the Inter-American Development Bank. This financing has been violently interrupted.

In the past decade, Chile received loans from the Agency for International Development of the Government of the United States (AID) totalling US$ 50 million a year.

We are not asking for those loans to be reinstated. The United States has the sovereign right to grant or not to grant foreign aid to any country. All we want to point out is that the drastic elimination of those credits has resulted in important restrictions in our balance of payments.

Upon taken office as President, my country had short-term credit lines from private US banks, destined to finance our foreign trade, that amounted to US$ 220 million. In a short period of time those credits were suspended and about US$ 190 million have been deducted, a sum we had to pay, since the respective operations were not renewed.

Just like most of the nations of Latin America, because of technological reasons and other factors, Chile must make important purchases of capital goods in the United States. Now, both the financing of the supplies and that normally provided by the Eximbank for this type of operation has also been suspended for us, putting us in the irregular position of having to purchase goods of that kind by paying in advance. This puts extraordinary pressure on our balance of payments.

Payments of loans contracted by Chile with agencies of the public sector of the United States before my Government took office, and which were being carried out then, have also been suspended; so we have to continue carrying out the corresponding projects making cash in hand purchases on the US market, because, once the projects are in full swing, it is impossible to replace the source of the respective imports. That is why it had been decided that the financing should come from US Government agencies.

As a result of the operations directed against the sale of copper in the nations of Western Europe, our short-term operations with private banks on that continent, mainly based on payment of that metal, have been greatly blocked. This has resulted in more than US$ 20 million in credit lines not being renewed, the suspension of financial negotiations for more than US$ 200 million that were almost complete, and the creation of a climate that blocks the normal handling of our purchases in those countries and acutely distorts all our activities in the field of external financing.

This financial stranglehold of a brutal nature, given the characteristics of the Chilean economy, has resulted in a severe limitations of our possibilities to purchase equipment, spare parts, supplies, food and medicine. Every Chilean is suffering the consequences of those measures, which bring suffering and grief into the daily life of all and, naturally, make themselves felt in internal political life.

What I have described means that the nature of the international agencies has been distorted. Their utilization as instruments of the bilateral policy of any of their member states, regardless of how powerful it may be, is legally and morally unacceptable. It means putting pressures on an economically weak country and punishing a nation for its decision to regain control over its basic resources. It is a premeditated form of intervention in the internal affairs of a nation. This is what we call imperialist arrogance.

Distinguished representatives, you know this and you cannot forget it. All this has been repeatedly condemned by resolutions of the United Nations.

CHILE ATTACKED BY TRANSNATIONAL COMPANIES

Not only do we suffer the financial blockade, we are also the victims of clear aggression. Two firms that are part of the central nucleus of the large transnational companies that sunk their claws into my country, the International Telegraph and Telephone Company and the Kennecott Copper Corporation, tried to run our political life.

ITT, a huge corporation whose capital is greater than the budget of several Latin American nations put together and greater than that of some industrialized countries, began, from the very moment that the people's movement was victorious in the elections of September 1970, a sinister action to keep me from taking office as President.

Between September and November of 1970, terrorist actions that were planned outside of my country took place there, with the aid of internal fascist groups. All this led to the murder of General Rene Schneider Chereau, Commander in Chief of the Army, a just man and a great soldier who symbolized the constitutionalism of the armed forces of Chile.

In March of this year, the documents that denounced the relationship between those sinister aims and the ITT were made public. This company has admitted that in 1970 it even made suggestions to the Government of the United States that it intervene in political events in Chile. The documents are genuine, nobody has dared deny them.

Last July the world learned with amazement of different aspects of a new plan of action that ITT had presented to the US Government in order to overthrow my Government in a period of six months. I have with me the document, dated in October 1971, that contains the 18-point plan that was talked about. They wanted to strangle us economically, carry out diplomatic sabotage, create panic among the population and cause social disorder so that when the Government lost control, the armed forces would be driven to eliminate the democratic regime and impose a dictatorship.

While the ITT was working out this plan, its representatives went through the motions of negotiating a formula for the Chilean state to take over ITT's share in the Chilean telephone company. From the first days of my administration, we had started talks to purchase the telephone company that ITT controlled, for reasons of national security.

On two occasions I received high officials of the firm. My Government acted in good faith in the discussions. On the other hand, ITT refused to accept payment at prices that had been set in keeping with the verdict of international experts. It posed difficulties for a rapid and fair solution, while clandestinely it was trying to unleash chaos in my country.

ITT's refusal to accept a direct agreement and knowledge of its sneaky manoeuvres has forced us to send to Congress a bill calling for its nationalization.

The will of the Chilean people to defend the democratic regime and the progress of its revolution, the loyalty of the armed forces to their country and its laws have caused these sinister plots to fail.

Distinguished representatives, before the conscience of the World I accuse ITT of trying to provoke a civil war in my country -the supreme state of disintegration for a country. This is what we call imperialist intervention.

Chile now faces a danger whose solution does not only depend on national will, but on a whole series of external elements. I am talking about the action of the Kennecott Copper Corporation.

Our constitution says that disputes caused by nationalizations must be solved by a court that, just like all the others in my country, is independent and sovereign in its decisions. Kennecott Copper accepted its jurisdiction and for a year it appeared before that tribunal. Its appeal was not accepted, and it decided to use its considerable power to deprive us of the benefits of our copper exports and put pressure on the Government of Chile. In September, it went so far in its arrogance as to demand the embargo of the payment of these exports in courts in France, Holland and Sweden. It will surely try the same thing in other countries. The basis for this action cannot be more unacceptable from the judicial and moral points of view.

Kennecott would have the courts of other nations, that have absolutely nothing to do with the problems or the negotiations between the Chilean state and the Kennecott Copper Corporation, decide that a sovereign act of our Government - carried out in response to a mandate of the highest authority, like that of the political constitution, and supported by all the Chilean people - is null and void. This attempt of theirs is in contradiction to basic principles of international law by virtue of which the natural resources of a country, especially those which constitute its livelihood, belong to the nation and it can dispose of them at will. There is no universally accepted international law or, in this case, specific treaty, which provides for that. The world community, organized under the principles of the United Nations, does not accept an interpretation of international law, subordinated to the interests of capitalism, that will lead the courts of any foreign country to back up a structure of economic relations at the service of the above-mentioned economic system. If that were the case, there would be a violation of a fundamental principle of international life: that of non-intervention in the internal affairs of a state, as was explicitly recognized at the third UNCTAD.

We are guided by international law repeatedly accepted by the United Nations, especially in resolution 1803 (XVIII) of the General Assembly; norms that have just been reinforced by the trade and development board, based itself on the charges my country made against Kennecott. The respective resolution reaffirmed the sovereign right of all states to freely dispose of their natural resources, and declared in application of this principle, that the nationalization carried out by states to regain control over those resources are an expression of their sovereign powers. Every state must set the standards for those measures and the disputes that may arise as a result are the exclusive concern of its courts, without prejudice to resolution 1803 of the General Assembly. This resolution allows the intervention of extra-national jurisdictions under exceptional conditions and as long as there is an agreement between sovereign states and other interested parties.

This is the only acceptable thesis of the United Nations. It is the only one that is in keeping with its philosophy and principles. It is the only one that can protect the rights of the weak against the abuses of the strong.

Since it could not be any other way, in the courts of Paris we have obtained the lifting of the embargo that had been in effect on the payment of a shipment of our copper. We will continue to ceaselessly defend the exclusive jurisdiction of Chilean courts over any dispute resulting from the nationalization of our basic resource.

For Chile, this is not only an important matter of judicial interpretation. It is a problem of sovereignty and, even more, of survival.

Kennecott's aggression inflicts grave damage on our economy. Just the direct difficulties imposed on the marketing of copper have resulted in the loss of many millions of dollars for Chile in the last two months alone. But that isn't all. I have already discussed the effects linked to the blocking of my country's financial operations with the banks of Western Europe. There is also an evident effort to create a climate of distrust among the buyers of our main export product, but this will fail.

The objectives of this imperialist firm are now going even further than that, because in the long run it cannot expect any political or legal power to deprive Chile of what rightfully belongs to her. It wants to bring us to our knees, but this will never happen.

The aggression of the big capitalist firms seeks to block the emancipation of the people. It represents a direct attack on the economic interests of the workers in the concrete case against Chile.

The Chilean people are a people that have reached the political maturity to decide by a majority the replacement of the capitalist economic system by a socialist one. Our political regime has institutions that have been open enough to channel that revolutionary will without violent clashes. It is my duty to warn this assembly that the reprisals and the blockade, aimed at producing contradictions and the resultant economic distortions, threaten to have repercussions on peace and internal coexistence in my country. They will not attain their evil objectives. The great majority of Chileans will find the way to resist them in a patriotic and dignified manner. What I said at the beginning will always be valid: our history, land and man are joined in a great national feeling.

THE PHENOMENON OF THE TRANSNATIONAL CORPORATIONS

At the third UNCTAD I was able to discuss the phenomenon of the transnational corporations. I mentioned the great growth in their economic power, political influence and corrupting action. That is the reason for the alarm with which world opinion should react in the face of a reality of this kind. The power of these corporations is so great that it goes beyond all borders. The foreign investments of US companies alone reached US$ 32,000 million. Between 1950 and 1970 they grew at a rate of 10 per cent a year, while that nation's exports only increased by 5 per cent. They make huge profits and drain off tremendous resources from the developing countries.

In just one year, these firms withdrew profits from the Third World that represented net transfers in their favour of US$ 1,743 million: US$ 1,013 million from Latin America; US$ 280 million from Africa; US$ 376 million from the Far East; and US$ 74 million from the Middle East. Their influence and their radius of action are upsetting the traditional trade practices of technological transfer among states, the transmission of resources among nations and labour relations.

We are faced by a direct confrontation between the large transnational corporations and the states. The corporations are interfering in the fundamental political, economic and military decisions of the states. The corporations are global organizations that do not depend on any state and whose activities are not controlled by, nor are they accountable to any parliament or any other institution representative of the collective interest. In short, all the world political structure is being undermined. The dealer's don't have a country. The place where they may be does not constitute any kind of link; the only thing they are interested in is where they make profits. This is not something I say; they are Jefferson's words.

The large transnational firms are prejudicial to the genuine interests of the developing countries and their dominating and uncontrolled action is also carried out in the industrialized countries, where they are based. This has recently been denounced in Europe and in the United States and resulted in a US Senate investigation. The developed nations are just as threatened by this danger as the underdeveloped ones. It is a phenomenon that has already given rise to the growing mobilization of organized workers including the large trade union organizations that exist in the world. Once again the action of the international solidarity of workers must face a common enemy: imperialism.

In the main, it was those acts that led the Economic and Social Council of the United Nations -following the denunciation madeby Chile- to unanimously approve, last July, a resolution that called for a group of world figures to meet and study the effects and function of transnational corporations in the process of development, especially in the developing countries, and their repercussions on international relations, and present recommendations for appropriate international action.

Ours is not an isolated or a unique problem. It is the local expression of a reality that overwhelms us, a reality that covers Latin America and the Third World. In varying degrees of intensity, with unique features, all the peripheral countries are threatened by something similar.

The spokesman for the African group at the Trade and Development Board a few weeks ago announced the position of those countries towards the denunciation made by Chile of Kennecott's aggresion, reporting that his group fully supported Chile, because it was a problem which did not affect only one nation but, potentially, all of the developing world. These words have great value, because they represent the recognition of an entire continent that through the Chilean case, a new stage in the battle between imperialism and the weak countries of the Third World is being waged.

THE COUNTRIES OF THE THIRD WORLD

The battle in defence of natural resources is but a part of the battle being waged by the countries of the Third World against underdevelopment. There is a very clear dialectical relationship: imperialism exists because underdevelopment exists; underdevelopment exists because imperialism exists. The aggression we are being made the object of today makes the fulfilment of the promises made in the last few years as to a new large- scope action aimed at overcoming the conditions of underdevelopment and want in the nations of Africa, Asia and Latin America appear illusory. Two years ago, on the occasion of the 25th anniversary of the founding of the United Nations, the UN General Assembly solemnly proclaimed the strategy for a second decade of development. In keeping with this strategy, all UN member states pledged to spare no efforts to transform, via concrete measures, the present unfair international division of labour and to close the vast economic and technological gap that separates the wealthy countries from the developing ones.

We have seen that none of those aims ever became a reality. On the contrary, the situation has worsened.

Thus, the markets of the industrialized countries have remained as tightly closed as they ever were to the basic products - chiefly the agricultural products - of the developing countries and the index of protectionist measures is on the increase. The terms of exchange continue to deteriorate, the system of generalized preferences for the exportation of our manufactured and semi-manufactured goods has never been put into effect by the nation whose market - considering its volume- offered the best perspectives and there are no indications that this will be done in the immediate future.

The transfer of public financial resources, rather than reaching 0.7 per cent of the gross national product of the developed nations, has dropped from 0.34 to 0.24 per cent. The debt contracted by the developing countries, which was already enormous by the beginning of this year, has skyrocketed to between $70 and $75 thousand million in only a few months. The sums for loan services paid by those countries, which represent an intolerable drain for them, have been to a great measure the result of the conditions and terms of the loans. In 1970 these services increased 18 per cent, and in 1971, 20 per cent -more than twice the mean rate for the 1960 decade.

This is the drama of underdevelopment and of the countries which have not stood up for their rights, which have not demanded respect for their rights and defended, through a vigorous collective action, the price of their raw materials and basic products and have not confronted the threats and aggressions by neo-imperialism.

We are potentially wealthy countries and yet we live a life of poverty. We go here and there, begging for credits and aid and yet we are - a paradox typical of the capitalist economic system - great exporters of capital.

LATIN AMERICA AND UNDERDEVELOPMENT

Latin America, as part of the developing world, forms part of the picture I have just described. Together with Asia, Africa and the socialist countries, she has waged many battles in the last few years to change the structure of the economic and commercial relations with the capitalist world, to replace the unfair and discriminatory economic and monetary order created in Bretton Woods at the end of World War II.

It is true that there are differences in the national income of many of the countries in our region and that of the countries on other continents, and even among countries that could be considered as relatively less developed among the underdeveloped countries.

However, such differences - which many mitigate by comparing them with the national product of the industrialized world - do not keep Latin America out of the vast neglected and exploited sector of humanity. The consensus at Vina del Mar, in 1969, affirmed these coincidences and defined, pointed out clearly and indicated the scope of the region's economic and social backwardness and the external factors that determined it, pointing out the great injustices that are being committed against the region under the disguise of cooperation and aid. I say this because large cities in Latin America, admired by many, hide the drama of hundreds of thousands of human beings living in marginal towns that are the product of unemployment and sub-employment. These beautiful cities hide the deep contrast between small groups of privileged individuals and the great masses whose nutrition and health indexes are the lowest.

It is easy to see why our Latin American continent shows such a high rate of infant mortality and illiteracy, with 13 million people out of jobs and more than 50 million doing only occasional work.

More than 20 million Latin American do not use money even as a means of exchange.

No regime, no government has been able to solve the great deficit in housing, labour, food and health. On the contrary, the deficit increases with every passing year in keeping with the population increase. If this situation continues, what will happen when there are more than 600 million of us by the end of the century?

The situation is even more dramatic in Asia and Africa, whose PER CAPITA income is even lower and whose process of development shows an even greater weakness.

It is not always noticed that the Latin American subcontinent - whose wealth potential is simply enormous - has become the principal field of action of economic imperialism for the last 30 years. Recent data given by the International Monetary Fund shows that private investment by the developed countries in Latin America shows a deficit against Latin America of $9,000 million between 1960 and 1970. In a word, that amount represents a net contribution of capital from our region to the wealthy world in one decade.

Chile is completely in solidarity with the rest of Latin America, without exception. For this reason, it favours and fully respects the policy of non-intervention and self-determination, which we apply on a worldwide scale. We enthusiastically foster the increase of our economic and cultural relations. We are in favour of the complementing and the integration of our economies. Hence, we work with enthusiasm within the framework of LAFTA and, as an initial step, for the creation of the Andean countries' common market, which unites us with Bolivia, Colombia, Peru and Ecuador.

Latin America has left the era of protest behind her. Needs and statistics contributed to an increased awareness. Reality has shattered all ideological barriers. All attempts at division and isolation have been defeated and there is an ardent desire to coordinate the offensive in defence of the interests of the countries on the continent and the other developing countries.

Those who make peaceful revolution impossible make violent revolution inevitable. These are not my words. I simply share the same opinion. The words are those of John F. Kennedy.

CHILE IS NOT ALONE

Chile is not alone. All attempts to isolate her from the rest of Latin America and the world have failed. On the contrary, Chile has been the object of endless demonstrations of solidarity and support. The ever- increasing condemnation of imperialism; the respect that the efforts of the people of Chile deserve; and the response to our policy of friendship with all the nations of the world, were all instrumental in defeating the attempts to surround our country with a ring of hostility.

In Latin America, all the plans for economic and cultural cooperation or integration, plans of which we form part on both the regional and subregional level, have continued to take on strength at an accelerated pace. As a result, our trade - particularly with Argentina, Mexico and the countries of the Andean Pact - has increased considerably.

The joint support of the Latin American countries in world and regional forums in favour of the principles of free determination over natural resources has remained firm as a rock. And, in response to the recent attacks against our sovereignty, we have been the object of demonstrations of complete solidarity. To all of these countries, we express our most deep-felt gratitude.

Socialist Cuba, which is suffering the rigours of blockade, has always given us her revolutionary solidarity.

On the world scale, I must point out very especially that we have enjoyed the full solidarity of the socialist countries in Europe and Asia from the very beginning. The great majority of the world community did us the honour of electing Santiago as the seat of the third UNCTAD meeting and has welcomed with great interest our invitation to be the site of the next world conference on rights to the sea - an invitation which I reiterate on this occasion.

The non-aligned countries' foreign ministers meeting, held in Georgetown, Guyana, in September, publicly expressed its determined support in response to the aggression of which we are being made the object by Kennecott Copper.

The CIPEC, an organization of coordination established by the main copper- exporting countries - Peru, Zaire, Zambia and Chile - which met recently in Santiago, at the ministers' level, at my suggestion, to analyse the situation of aggression against my country created by Kennecott Copper, has just adopted a number of resolutions and recommendations of vast importance to the various states. These resolutions and recomendations constitute an unreserved support of our position and an important step taken by countries of the Third World in defence of trade of their basic products.

The resolutions will no doubt constitute important material for the second commission. But I would like to refer at this moment to the categorical declaration to the effect that any action that may impede or obstruct the exercise of a country's sovereign right to dispose freely of its antural resources constitutes an economic attack. Needless to say, the Kennecott actions against Chile constitute an economic aggression and, therefore, the ministers agreed on asking their respective governments to suspend all economic and commercial relations with the firm and state that disputes on compensation in case of nationalization are the exclusive concern of those states which adopt such measures.

However, the most significant thing is that it was resolved 'to establish a permanent mechanism of protection and solidarity' in relation to copper. Mechanisms such as this one, together with the OPEC, which operates in the field of petroleum, are the germ of what would be an organization which would include all the countries of the Third World to protect and defend all basic products - including the mining, petroleum and agricultural fields.

The great majority of the countries in Western Europe, from the Scandinavian countries in the extreme north to Spain in the extreme south, have been cooperating with Chile, and their understanding has meant a form of support to us. It is thanks to this understanding that we have renegotiated our foreign debt.

And, lastly, we have been deeply moved by the solidarity of the world's working class, expressed by its great trade union central organizations and demonstrated in actions of great significance, such as the port workers of Le Havre and Rotterdam's refusal to unload copper from Chile whose payment has been arbitrarily and unfairly embargoed.

Salvador Allende on Latin America October 3 1973

People of the University--I use this phrase to refer to all educational workers, from the President of this University to the most humble comrade:

Students:

How difficult it is for me to express how I have felt in this brief yet long time of fellowship with the Mexican people--with your government. How can we express our thanks for what we, the members of the Chilean delegation, have received in support and in expressions of solidarity with our people in the hard struggle that we are fighting?

I, perhaps more than others, know perfectly well that this attitude of the Mexican people grows out of your past. We remember here how Chile was at the side of Juarez, the leader of Mexico's independence who extended the struggle across the whole continent. We understand perfectly well that in addition to these common roots, a common struggle against the conquistadores, Mexico was the first Latin American country, which in 1938, led by a distinguished man of this land and of Latin America, President Lazaro Cardenas, nationalized oil.

Because of that act, you, the Mexican people, learned immediately of the coward's attack, you had cause to feel a deep, profound feeling for your fatherland. Because of that act for a long time you suffered under the attack of the oil interests wounded by the nationalization. Because of that act, you, more than the other peoples of this continent, understand the hour of Chile, that it is the same hour that you experienced in 1938 and in the following years. Because of that the solidarity of Mexico was born out of its own experience and extends itself fraternally to Chile, and Chile is now following the same route to freedom that you followed.

PRESIDENT ECHEVERRIA spoke well when he advised me that in this trip it would be useful for me to visit a province. He told me about Jalisco and he spoke to me of Guadalajara and its University. I thanked him then, and now--certainly--I thank him more. Because we have received the friendly affection of the Mexican people, of your women and of your men. What can be more important than to be in touch with the young people, and feel how they react strongly and vibrantly, with a clear revolutionary and anti-imperialist conscience?

Since the moment I arrived here, I understood perfectly well the spirit that exists here. Coming only as a messenger of my country, I could immediately sense your feelings from seeing the posters that greeted my arrival.

This is no traditional University: this is--as many other universities on this continent are not--a University that has been reformed. I believe that this is a University that is engaged with the people, with changes, with the struggle for economic independence and for the complete independence of our people.

I once went to a university--it has been many years, of course, don't ask me how many--but I got a college education. I went not in search of a diploma because I was a student leader and I was expelled from the university. I can speak to students from across the years, but I know that you know that there is no generation gap--there are young old people and old young people, and I place myself in the latter category.

But there are young old people who do not understand that to be a university student, for instance, is an extraordinary privilege in the enormous majority of the countries of our continent. Those young old people believe that the university has been created to train technicians and they think that they should be satisfied with merely acquiring a professional title. The degree gives them social status and boosts them on their way up the social ladder. Caramba, how terribly dangerous, the degree is, an instrument that gives them more income and better living conditions than the majority of the rest of our fellow citizens.

AND THESE YOUNG old, if they are architects, for example, don't ask themselves how much housing is needed in our countries, or sometimes, not even in their own country. There are students, who, following strict liberal criteria, make an honest living from their profession, but basically, they still think only of their own interests.

Back in Chile, there are many doctors--and I am a doctor--who do not understand or who do not want to understand that good health can be bought; and that there are thousands and thousands and thousands of men and women in Latin America who cannot afford good health. These doctors do not want to understand, for example, that more poverty means more sickness, and, in turn, more sickness means more poverty, and, therefore, if they perform their duty well for the patient who can pay, they do not think of the thousands of people who cannot afford to go to their offices. There are only a few doctors who struggle to establish government agencies to bring good health to the masses.

In the same way, there are teachers who are not worried at the fact that there are also hundreds and thousands of children and young people who cannot enter school. The statistics of Latin America are dramatic in their painful reality.

Today, almost all of our countries have been politically independent for more than one and one-half centuries, but where is the data that shows how much of our dependency and exploitation remains? Although potentially rich countries, the vast majority of our nations are poor.

In Latin America, a continent with more than 220 million inhabitants, there are 100 million illiterate or semiliterate people. In this country there are more than 30 million unemployed people, and, taking into account those who work only occasionally, the figure rises to over 60 million.

ON OUR CONTINENT between 53 and 57 per cent of the population suffers from malnutrition. Latin America lacks more than 28 million housing units.

Under these circumstances, one might ask, what will happen to the young people?--because this is a young continent; 51 per cent of the population of Latin America is under 27. It is a tragedy that I can say--and I wish that I was wrong--that no government, including, certainly, mine and those of my predecessors in Chile, has solved the problems of the majority of our continent regarding unemployment, malnutrition, housing and health care. To say nothing of better recreation and shorter working hours and more holidays for the poor.

Our nations have been surrounded and imprisoned by poverty and ignorance for one and one-half centuries. From the pain and suffering of the masses surge aspirations of reaching higher levels of material life, existence and culture. It is antihuman, it is anti-social, to deny this to man.

If these figures are bad today, what will happen if things don't change by the time there are 360 or 600 million of us? In a continent where the demographic explosion is compensating for the high infant mortality rate, our nations defend themselves. But despite this, the population of our countries increases vigorously. It is true that technological advance in the field of medicine has risen, and these advances have improved living conditions somewhat. Our average life expectancy has also risen, although, certainly, it is still much inferior to that of the capitalist industrial countries and the socialist countries.

But no government on this continent --there are a few democratic ones, there are some more pseudodemocratic ones, and there are even a few dictatorships--no government has been able to overcome these great problems. Some, especially the democratic ones, have made indisputably laudable efforts, laudable because they listen to the voices of protest, the aspirations of their people. They seek to advance in this frustrating attempt, in order to stop these problems from weighing heavily on our lives.

AND WHY DOES all of this happen? Because the inmense majority of our countries are single producers: we are the countries of chocolate, bananas, coffee, tin, oil or copper. We are countries that produce raw materials and import manufactured articles: we sell low and buy high.

By buying high, we are paying the high salaries of the technician, the clerk and the worker in the industrialized countries. Because our primary resources are in the hands of foreign capital, we ignore marketing strategies, we don't set prices or levels of production. We have had this experience with copper and you have had it with oil.

The great finance capitalists look at our countries for the possibility of obtaining great profits. Many times, because of the guilty complacency of people who don't want to understand the meaning of patriotism, they find those opportunities for gain.

But what is imperialism, young comrades? It occurs when the concentration of capital in the industrialized countries reaches the stage of finance capital and abandons investments in the metropolitan economies in order to invest in our countries. This capital, that has little use in its own metropolis, is therefore able to earn huge profits in our lands. These contracts are made between companies that are based here and the companies that own them from beyond our frontiers. The agreements are beyond our control.

Thus, we are countries that cannot take advantage of the surplus of our own production. This is a fact that this continent well knows--not because of social agitators with political last names, like the one I have of socialist--but because of figures provided by committees of the United Nations. In the past decade, Latin America exported more capital than it imported.

IN THIS WAY, a reality common to the immense majority of our countries has been produced: we are potentially rich, but we live poor. In order to continue living, we borrow. But at the same time we export capital. This is a typical paradox in the international relations of the capitalist system.

It is indespensable to understand what this system means to us. Internationally powerful countries base the growth and strength of their economies on our poverty and financially strong countries need our raw materials in order to remain strong. The reality of the market and price structure forces the nations of this and other continents deeply into debt, to the point where the debt of the countries of the Third World reaches the fantastic figure of $95 billion dollars.

My country is a democratic one with sturdy institutions, a country whose parliament has functioned for 160 years and where the armed forces--the same as in Mexico--are professional armed forces, who respect the laws and the popular will. My country is the second largest producer of copper in the world, the biggest strip mine in the world, and the biggest underground mine in the world. My country has run up a per capita foreign debt second only to Israel, which can be considered a nation at war. I must this year pay $420 million--which is 30 per cent of my government's income--for the interest and amortization alone. It is easy to understand why it is impossible that this situation can continue and this reality be maintained.

Add to that the fact that the powerful countries set the rules of commercial trade--they control transport, they impose the insurance rates, they loan us money with the stipulation that a high percentage of that money be re-invested in the metropolis. Besides, we suffer the consequences when the powerful countries or the most powerful country feels the need to devalue its currency. We pay the consequences. If the international money market trembles in the industrial countries, the repercussions here are much stronger, much harder, they weigh more heavily on our people. If the price of raw materials falls, the price of manufactured articles, and even of imported food, goes up. When the price of food goes up, we discover that there are customs barriers which impede products from those of our countries that export food from entering consumer markets in the industrial countries.

Salvador Allende

Last Words to the Nation

My friends,

Surely this will be the last opportunity for me to address you. The Air Force has bombed the towers of Radio Portales and Radio Corporación.

My words do not have bitterness but disappointment. May they be a moral punishment for those who have betrayed their oath: soldiers of Chile, titular commanders in chief, Admiral Merino, who has designated himself Commander of the Navy, and Mr. Mendoza, the despicable general who only yesterday pledged his fidelity and loyalty to the Government, and who also has appointed himself Chief of the Carabineros [national police].

Given these facts, the only thing left for me is to say to workers: I am not going to resign!

Placed in a historic transition, I will pay for loyalty to the people with my life. And I say to them that I am certain that the seed which we have planted in the good conscience of thousands and thousands of Chileans will not be shriveled forever.

They have strength and will be able to dominate us, but social processes can be arrested neither by crime nor force. History is ours, and people make history.

Workers of my country: I want to thank you for the loyalty that you always had, the confidence that you deposited in a man who was only an interpreter of great yearnings for justice, who gave his word that he would respect the Constitution and the law and did just that. At this definitive moment, the last moment when I can address you, I wish you to take advantage of the lesson: foreign capital, imperialism, together with the reaction, created the climate in which the Armed Forces broke their tradition, the tradition taught by General Schneider and reaffirmed by Commander Araya, victims of the same social sector which will today be in their homes hoping, with foreign assistance, to retake power to continue defending their profits and their privileges.

I address, above all, the modest woman of our land, the campesina who believed in us, the worker who labored more, the mother who knew our concern for children. I address professionals of Chile, patriotic professionals, those who days ago continued working against the sedition sponsored by professional associations, class-based associations that also defended the advantages which a capitalist society grants to a few.

I address the youth, those who sang and gave us their joy and their spirit of struggle. I address the man of Chile, the worker, the farmer, the intellectual, those who will be persecuted, because in our country fascism has been already present for many hours -- in terrorist attacks, blowing up the bridges, cutting the railroad tracks, destroying the oil and gas pipelines, in the face of the silence of those who had the obligation to protect them. They were committed. History will judge them.

Surely Radio Magallanes will be silenced, and the calm metal instrument of my voice will no longer reach you. It does not matter. You will continue hearing it. I will always be next to you. At least my memory will be that of a man of dignity who was loyal to [inaudible] the workers.

The people must defend themselves, but they must not sacrifice themselves. The people must not let themselves be destroyed or riddled with bullets, but they cannot be humiliated either.

Workers of my country, I have faith in Chile and its destiny. Other men will overcome this dark and bitter moment when treason seeks to prevail. Go forward knowing that, sooner rather than later, the great avenues will open again where free men will walk to build a better society.

Long live Chile! Long live the people! Long live the workers!

These are my last words, and I am certain that my sacrifice will not be in vain, I am certain that, at the very least, it will be a moral lesson that will punish felony, cowardice, and treason.

Santiago de Chile, 11 September 1973